*Planning
library
service*

Planning
library
service

Bob McKee MA PhD DipLib ALA MIInfSc

CLIVE BINGLEY   LONDON

© Bob McKee 1989

Published by
Library Association Publishing Ltd
7 Ridgmount Street
London WC1E 7AE

First published 1989

British Library Cataloguing in Publication Data

McKee, Bob
    Planning library service.
    1. Libraries. Management
    I. Title
    025.1

    ISBN 0-85157-424-6

Typeset in 11/12pt Baskerville by Library Association Publishing Ltd
Printed and Bound in Great Britain by
Redwood Burn Limited, Trowbridge, Wiltshire.

Contents

Foreword

This book draws on four years thinking and discussion with students and practitioners while teaching in the Department of Librarianship and Information Studies at Birmingham Polytechnic, England.

It attempts to fill a gap in the literature by providing a current textbook giving an overview of the main areas usually covered in courses on library management. Throughout – in order to avoid tortuous elongations – the word 'library' is taken to include concepts of 'information' service.

Although it is based in UK experience, the issues raised and principles discussed have international relevance. While writing the book, I made two visits to the United States, and was struck by the close similarity between UK concerns and those emerging in the USA. I have tried to incorporate this American experience into the text.

The book is intended to be useful not only to students, but also to practitioners who are entering, or already working in, positions with some managerial responsibility.

The core elements and principles of management are transferable to all types of organization. The detail and the examples used in this book relate to libraries, but, because library management encompasses many of the issues currently affecting managers in all types of organization, it is hoped that the book will find a wider readership amongst those studying, practising, or simply interested in management in general.

This book marks the end of a chapter in my career: while writing it, I left my teaching post at Birmingham Polytechnic to return to the practice of library management. I take this opportunity to thank many colleagues at Birmingham Polytechnic

vii

– past and present, staff and students – for their help, support and friendship. Teaching is a responsibility and also a privilege. It has been, for me, an immensely enjoyable and fulfilling experience.

The book is dedicated to all those former students who recognize, in these pages, the occasional glimmer of a half-forgotten lecture or seminar on the third floor of Dawson Building. Thanks for the memories.

Bob McKee
Balsall Common
January 1989

Acknowledgements

Thanks to the many librarians and managers who have, unwittingly, contributed to the development of my thinking in meetings, conferences, seminars and bars over a decade of animated discussion.

Thanks in particular to Rosemary Raddon who read the text in draft form and provided a number of useful comments.

Thanks also to the staff of the British Library Information Science Service (BLISS) whose swift and efficient performance showed many of the qualities discussed in this book – particularly 'value for money' and a 'customer first' approach to service.

Responsibility for the final text rests, of course, with me.

For excerpts reproduced in this book, acknowledgement is made to the following sources:

- *Advancing with knowledge: the British Library strategic plan, 1985 – 1990*, British Library, 1985.
- Barbara H. Baskin and Karen H. Harris (eds.), *The mainstreamed library: issues, ideas, innovations,* Chicago, American Library Association, 1982.
- John Blagden, *Do we really need libraries?*, Bingley, 1980.
- Kenneth Blanchard and Spenser Johnson, *The one minute manager*, Fontana/Collins, 1983.
- Peter Brophy, *Management information and decision support systems in libraries*, Gower, 1986.
- John Cowley, *Personnel management in libraries*, Bingley, 1982.
- Sandy Dolnick, *Friends of libraries sourcebook*, Chicago, American Library Association, 1980.
- Peter Drucker, *The practice of management*, Heinemann, 1955.

- Edward Dudley (ed.), *The development of national library and information services*, Library Association, 1983.
- *Financing our public library service: four subjects for debate*, Cm.324, HMSO, 1988.
- *The future development of libraries and information services: progress through planning and partnership; report by the Library and Information Services Council*, Library Information Series no.14, HMSO, 1986.
- *The future development of libraries and information services: working together within a national framework*, DES/OAL, Library Information Series no.12, HMSO, 1982.
- *Getting closer to the public*, Luton, Local Government Training Board, 1987.
- Charles B. Handy, *Understanding organizations*, third edition, Harmondsworth, Penguin Books, 1985.
- Peter Lawrence, *Invitation to management*, Oxford, Blackwell, 1986.
- David Liddle, *What the public library boss does*, Newcastle-under-Lyme, Association of Assistant Librarians, 1985.
- Ian Lovecy, *Automating library procedures: a survivor's handbook*, Library Association, 1984.
- Tom Lupton, *Management and the social sciences*, third edition, Harmondsworth, Penguin Books, 1983.
- Anne J. Matthews, *Communicate! A librarian's guide to interpersonal relations*, Chicago, American Library Association, 1983.
- Charles R. McClure, *et al., Planning and role setting for public libraries: a manual of options and procedures*, Chicago, American Library Association, 1987.
- *Measuring up: consumer assessment of local authority services; paper three, public libraries*, National Consumer Council, 1986.
- Henry Mintzberg, *The nature of managerial work*, New York, Harper and Row, 1973.
- Vernon E. Palmour, *et al., A planning process for public libraries*, Chicago, American Library Association, 1980.
- Tom Peters and Nancy Austin, *A passion for excellence: the leadership difference*, Fontana/Collins, 1986.
- *Report by the Minister for the Arts on library and information matters during 1987*, HC 332, HMSO, 1988.
- Philip Rosenberg, *Cost finding for public libraries: a manager's*

handbook, Chicago, American Library Association, 1985.
- Rosemary Stewart, *The reality of management*, Second edition, Heinemann, 1985.
- Roger Stoakley, *Presenting the library service*, Bingley, 1982.

Note
Throughout the book I have tried to avoid gender stereotypes and so have not followed the convenient but sexist convention of using 'he' to cover 'she'. Unfortunately, I cannot say the same for some of the quotations used.

1 *Introduction*

The challenge of change: external forces
One of the favourite questions used by job interviewers is 'Where do you expect to be in five years time?' For many people, the question is out of date. They are working in jobs and industries that hardly existed a few years ago. Technology, and its impact on work, is one example of the rapid and pervasive change that is affecting all aspects of life.

The impact of technology is seen clearly in the changed landscape of libraries: the card catalogue replaced by a microfiche reader or computer terminal; the manual issue system with its trays of filing replaced by bar-coding and a light pen; the reference books supplemented by online workstations.

But, behind the scenes, libraries are being affected fundamentally by a number of external forces for change: particularly social, economic and political forces.

The function of library service is to meet the needs of potential customers. So the library manager has to respond to – indeed, to anticipate and plan for – change within the 'customer community'. In a public library, for example, changes in population (more pre-school children, more elderly people, etc.) and social conditions (more unemployment, a changing racial/cultural mix, etc.) should mean changes in the nature of service. Similarly, changes in the subjects taught and the methods of learning should mean changes in the services provided by an academic library.

Some librarians shy away from the term 'customer' because it hints at commerce (customers *pay* for things). But there are problematic connotations with many of the terms used by librarians to refer to the people who use – or might use – their services.

Borrowers, readers and *users* are redolent of a passive approach to service; a 'take it or leave it' attitude which provides a range of services for those who bother to find out about them and use them – but doesn't do much to actively discover what services might be needed or to promote those services. *Clients* has overtones of the traditional concept of the professional-client relationship, by which the client is dependent on and subordinate to the expertise and judgement of a 'professional'. In both cases, the service is supply-led; that is, the nature and extent of service is determined by the supplier.

The American term *patron* has never found favour in the UK, probably because the idea of being 'patronized' has pejorative overtones.

Inherent in the idea of someone giving their 'custom' to a service or product is the concept of choice; a customer is someone who chooses to use a particular service or product rather than doing something else. Libraries are only used by people who choose to use them – there is no compulsion or necessity as there is to attend classes or visit the doctor.

In the commercial context, a customer also has legal rights as a consumer. In the library context this is not the case (no one has – yet – taken a librarian to litigation for providing misleading information or out-of-date material), but the 'spirit' of the law can be applied; customers have expectations of a high quality of service delivery. Finally, as well as recognizing the element of personal choice and the need for high-quality service, the term carries with it an emphasis on the primacy of the customer – without the customer, there would be no service.

The concept of the customer – of choice and quality, of putting the customer first – leads to a market-led approach to service; that is, the nature and extent of service is determined by the demands, wants and needs of the customer community. To be successful, the market-led approach requires library managers to respond to – indeed, to anticipate – changes in the customer marketplace.

However, library managers operate within a framework of constraints determined by those people who are ultimately responsible for the library service – those to whom the manager is accountable. The structure of this 'governing framework' will differ for library managers in differing sectors: public service,

2

academic institutions, business corporations and so on. But the principle will remain the same. The broad lines of policy and resourcing will be determined by that governing framework, as will the organizational structure and 'culture' into which the library service must fit. One of the major challenges for library managers at senior level is to keep in balance the needs of customers (in terms of service delivery) and the requirements of the governing framework (in terms of policy objectives and resource limits).

Change in the nature or policies of the governing framework can have a major impact on library service. The most dramatic example of this is the industrial corporation, caught by the recession, which decides to weather the economic storm by reducing overheads and closing down 'marginal' activities – and so shuts down, or drastically reduces, library provision. Similarly, UK government policies of reducing public-sector spending and encouraging strategies of 'enterprise' and increased financial self-determination are having a significant impact on policy, resourcing and the management 'culture' of public libraries, academic libraries and the British Library. In the USA, strategies to reduce the Federal deficit will have a similar impact on publicly funded services.

Both the governing framework and the customer community are affected, directly or indirectly, by a number of external environments. For example, in the UK, one such environment which is having an increasing impact is Europe – the European Community's plans for a 'single European market' to come into effect in 1992.

The European Council of Ministers adopted a resolution recognizing the importance of libraries in September 1985 and the European Commission is working on a programme of action for libraries. A number of library-related projects using new technology have been set up, such as the attempt, using OSI (Open Systems Interconnection) protocols, to link together differing library automation systems; or the exchange and joint publication, using CD-ROM, of national bibliographies.

European Commission policy – and money – is beginning to drive some of the thinking within the UK library world, and not only in relation to the use of new information technologies. Clwyd, in North Wales, has received £262,050 from the European

Regional Development Fund for a library and tourist information centre in Rhyl, and £10,000 from the European Social Fund for library and information support to agriculture in the region.[1]

In the world of libraries, as in other areas, key external factors (social, economic, political and technological) are combining to produce an era of 'discontinuous' change on both sides of the Atlantic – that is, change that represents a radical shift away from the assumptions and preconceptions of previous eras so that the past and its precedents are no guide to the future. In public libraries, for example, suggestions of a fee-based leisure service or an income generating, high-tech, 'added value' information service represent a discontinuous shift away from the tradition of a 'free' and 'comprehensive' public service. The model of a service which channels resources to disadvantaged groups, to help redress what are perceived as structural inequalities in society, represents a discontinuous shift away from a passive, building-based library service, used mainly by the middle class.

Social change alters the nature of society's needs – including the ways in which libraries are used, and thus the defined purpose and stated priorities of library service. Technological change alters the tools – the systems and structures – by which purpose can be achieved and service delivered. Economic change alters the resources available, and political change alters the policy framework (including decisions about the ways in which resources are allocated). These external forces are summarized in Figure 1, and, for managers, one aspect of the challenge of change is the strategic thinking that is needed in order to take them into account.

The challenge of change: internal dynamics
Alongside external forces for change, there are also internal variables which the library manager has to take into account.

The size of an organization and the scale of its operation can fluctuate. In the UK, local government reorganization and the internal restructuring of local authorities has had considerable impact on the size and scope of the departments responsible for public library service. The move to larger administrative units (by creating directorates incorporating several service departments) has been counterbalanced, in some local authorities, by a move to 'decentralize' service down to local, neighbourhood level.

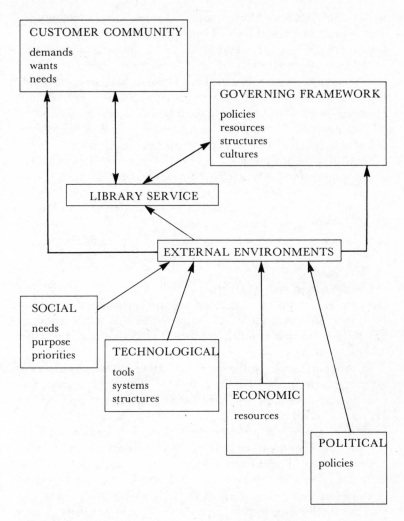

Figure 1: Library service in a context of change

In the academic and national library sectors, there have also been changes in size, resulting from mergers brought about by the creation of the polytechnics and the British Library.

Changes in size can produce changes in organizational structure, as can the search for new patterns of service provision.

In academic libraries, for example, changes in technology and educational methods have been paralleled by changes in organizational structure. Technological advance has reduced the need for on-site 'technical' services (for example, using an online bibliographical resource like the OCLC database reduces the need for on-site cataloguing) while the move to student-centred and resource-based learning methods has increased the need for 'reader' services: user education programmes, subject specialist librarians, involvement in curriculum development, etc.

Similarly, a number of public library departments, in attempting to develop a service which is more responsive to local people, have switched from a buildings-based organizational structure (a professional librarian at each service point) to a community-based 'team' approach (a team of professional librarians working together in a particular geographic area), or to a 'matrix' structure which combines elements of both these approaches.

Changes in size and structure clearly link to changes in the number and nature of staff. Staff are the key internal variable. In any organization there will be an element of staff turnover, and different people will bring different attributes and strengths – and weaknesses – into the organization.

In addition, staffing within an organization will reflect changing career patterns in the workforce at large. This is illustrated, for example, by developments in the career patterns and aspirations of women. With more women staying in work, or returning to work, and aspiring to a professionally satisfying career – allied to wider developments such as raised consciousness and a shift in stereotypical gender roles – there is increasing dissatisfaction with the patriarchal structures and macho attitudes which characterize much management thinking and activity. This has particular relevance for libraries where the vast majority of the workforce are women, but the majority of managers are men.

A further important internal variable – which tends to bring together considerations of size, structure and staffing – is that of style; the management style and set of shared values which helps determine the 'culture' of an organization, or unit. For example, an indicative list of contrasting styles might read:

formal	*informal*
conformist	*creative*
conservative	*innovative*
centralized	*delegated*
autocratic	*participative*
top down	*bottom up*

The culture of an organization and the style of its management permeate all aspects of the operation from seemingly small details (are people on first-name terms? who makes the coffee?) to the big issues: how are decisions made? how is risk-taking viewed? Figure 2 illustrates these interconnected internal variables. It has some kinship with the McKinsey 7-S Framework, popularized by Peters and Waterman,[2] which posits seven interdependent internal variables: structure, strategy, people, management style, systems and procedures, corporate culture, and corporate strengths or skills.

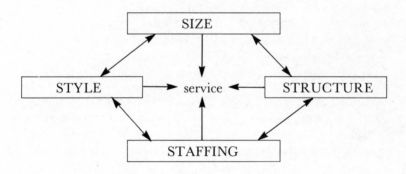

Figure 2: Internal variables

The internal dynamics of an organization – and the attitudes of the people within it – can create barriers to change. The power of the *status quo* means that there are always people with vested interests who benefit from, or feel comfortable with, the present way of doing things. Bureaucratic inertia is, in part, the cumulative impact of those individuals who will not, or cannot, or do not wish to make the effort that is required in order to produce internal change.

A particularly important challenge for library managers in the context of rapid external change is to develop organizations and individuals in ways which make them hospitable to that changing context. However, too much change – or change which is too swift or unsupported – can destroy. The challenge for management is to keep in balance the external forces for change and the internal dynamics of an organization; stimulating flexibility, encouraging innovation and creating a climate which is hospitable to change while, at the same time, maintaining stability, giving a clear sense of the organization's 'mission' or direction, and nurturing motivation and individual morale.

This last point raises the important distinction between *product* and *process*. Managers are concerned with *product* – achieving outcomes, accomplishing tasks. But they must also be concerned with *process*; not just *what* is done, but *how* it is done. It is impossible for an organization to sustain a healthy internal environment if managers do not give due attention to interpersonal processes centred on respect for the individual, support and counselling, team building, awareness of staff development needs, and recognition of personal career aspirations.

Enterprise and accountability: a change of approach

A key example of an external force for change is the policy of the UK government with regard to public-sector spending – a policy which may well be paralleled in the post-Reagan USA. A major thrust of that policy is to promote the concepts of 'enterprise' and 'accountability'. This approach can be contrasted with the traditional public-sector library culture as follows:

traditional	enterprising
dependent	self-reliant
income related to previous expenditure	income related to performance
'comprehensive . . .	priorities
. . . and efficient'	'value for money'
supply-led	market-led

There is a serious debate amongst librarians in Britain and in America as to whether the concepts in the right-hand column sit easily with the purpose and values of public service. However, these concepts are being applied in areas which are traditionally part of the state sector. Underlying them is the link between the enterprise culture, with its focus on self-determination and opportunism, and the concept of accountability.

Librarians and information scientists working in a business environment have always been required to account for their activities; to demonstrate the contribution made by their service to corporate objectives and profits. In a number of commercial organizations this is now reflected in the corporate financial structure with the library or information service no longer an area of expenditure to be simply subsumed into corporate overheads. The library becomes a separate accounting unit, charging other departments within the organization for their use of library services. It thus becomes possible to measure, in financial terms, the cost of library service and its contribution to corporate activity.

This pressure for accountability is now also strong in the public sector, expressed, for example, in the work of bodies like the Audit Commission, responsible for monitoring the 'economy, efficiency and effectiveness' of local government services in the UK.

The key catchphrase on both sides of the Atlantic is 'value for money'. The UK Minister for Arts and Libraries, Richard Luce, in his annual report to Parliament for 1987, stressed[3] how important it is ' . . . that library authorities should produce value for the money they spend and should be seen to be doing so'. The Minister is clear[4] on the mechanisms by which this can be achieved

> When library authorities are equipped to set meaningful objectives, cost the resources they put into the related services and measure their success, they will be in a much better position not only to obtain good value for money but to demonstrate to the public and to Parliament that they are doing so.

Accountability thus requires library managers to

- identify priorities and set (measurable) objectives and targets for service delivery.
- calculate the true cost of library functions and services.
- develop performance indicators which will measure the 'success' of the service.

Similar thinking (although from a professional rather than political perspective) lies behind the ALA's Public Library Development Program.

Enterprise and accountability come together in the concept of 'competitive tendering'. The basis of this is the commonplace idea that, rather than doing a job yourself, you might get someone else to do it for you – for a fixed fee and to agreed standards. So, rather than providing a service directly, an organization might choose to put that service out to 'competitive tender' and hire a contractor to provide the service. The organization becomes an enabler rather than a provider – a client, specifying standards and monitoring service. The mechanism of competitive tendering requires the client-organization to have clear objectives, costings and methods of performance measurement – and the consultative 'green paper' on public library financing, issued by the UK Government in February 1988, makes it clear[5] that: 'The Government would like to explore the scope for increasing library authority accountability by the discipline of competitive tendering.'

To cope with these issues of enterprise and accountability – in a context of rapid and discontinuous change – library managers are faced with a number of key strategic issues. An indicative agenda might include

- the need to prioritize service to particular customer-groups rather than attempting to offer a 'comprehensive' service with constrained resources.
- the need to develop internal information systems which demonstrate the quality and value of service and enable a judgement to be made about performance in relation to standards, objectives and targets, and costs.
- the need to develop decision-making structures to cope with priority-setting and performance evaluation.
- the need to assimilate technological developments where these are appropriate to the objectives of efficient and effective service delivery.
- the need to consider cooperation between library systems to provide a better coordinated and rationalized service: as is done by resource-sharing cooperatives; in the USA by multi-type networks;[6] and, in the UK, by Library and Information

10

Plans developed jointly by all types of library within a single geographic region.[7]

- the need to diversify the library's resource-base away from dependence on public funding or corporate overheads; for example, considering joint ventures between public-sector libraries and private-sector agencies in order to bring new information products and services to the marketplace.[8]

This is an agenda for strategic thinking, decision-making, and implementation which requires management ability of a high order. The challenge of change, the pressure for accountability and the emergence of the 'enterprise' culture all emphasize the fact that library services need to be proactive rather than passive; and thus need to be positively and effectively managed.

Definitions of management

But what is meant by *management* or *managing* or being a *manager*? Peter Lawrence[9] offers a useful working definition

Management is usually defined as getting things done with or through other people. It involves making decisions about objectives and means to achieve the ends set and more frequently making decisions to solve lots of problems that will otherwise frustrate the achievement of these objectives. Management is about planning and organising to get things done, and especially about coordinating, about bringing together, reconciling and integrating various activities or parts of the task that all contribute to the whole. It is also about controlling or making sure things are going according to plan, that objectives are being realised, and often a lot of thought and energy goes into generating information that will facilitate this control. The organisation in which this is all happening is made up of people, not mechanical parts, so that relations between people, communicating and maintaining commitment are all important.

This definition incorporates all the activities which are generally accepted as being characteristic of management. Essentially, it contains three elements.

First, there is the classic 'management cycle', a version of which is given in Figure 3. In Lawrence's definition the cycle has three

11

stages: planning (setting objectives and determining the means to achieve those objectives); organizing and coordinating (deploying resources and integrating activities); and controlling (setting up feedback systems to ensure that things are going to plan).

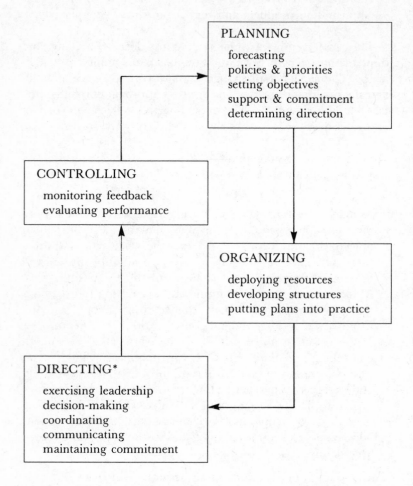

DIRECTING as the term is used in the theatre; leading, but also team building.

Figure 3: The management cycle

Second, there is the human dimension which Lawrence rightly emphasizes: the interplay between people, and also what Charles Handy[10] describes as the 'psychological contract' between individual and organization. Lawrence mentions interpersonal relations, communications and motivation ('maintaining commitment') as important elements in management. This reflects Peter Drucker's approach in his classic *The practice of management*[11] in which Drucker identifies five basic operations in the work of a manager

- setting objectives
- organizing
- motivating and communicating
- measuring
- developing people

Drucker uses a version of the classic management cycle (objectives, organizing, measuring; i.e. planning, organizing, control) and adds the human dimension, not just in terms of motivation and communication, but also in the important concept of 'developing people'.

While the 'management cycle' is a continuous process, it is not strictly cyclic in the sense of a structured flow from one function to the next. The reality of managing is not as orderly as the theory of management might suggest and the various activities in the cycle often blur and merge into each other. This is seen in the idea of 'organization'. In common speech the word is used in two senses: an 'organization' such as a business corporation or academic institution; and the act of 'organization', of getting things into order for a particular purpose. Within the management cycle – and bearing in mind that organizations are made up of people – the two meanings combine. An organization, from the management perspective, is not a static institution but an active, dynamic process.

Management, then, is a process – and the third element in Lawrence's definition indicates how that process manifests itself in the day-to-day activities of a manager. Management is about decision-making and problem-solving, both on the strategic level (setting objectives, allocating resources, determining strategies) and, more frequently, on the operational level ('making decisions

13

to solve lots of problems that will otherwise frustrate the achievement of these objectives').

Implicit in this part of Lawrence's definition is a contrast between the structured model of the 'management cycle' theory and a less structured, more fragmented, people-centred reality. A number of studies, by Lawrence[12] and others, show that the work of managing is very rarely orderly, controlled and reflective. Rather, it is highly active (going to meetings, touring the 'shop-floor') and interactive (talking to people in meetings, on-site and over the telephone). It is also fragmented, switching from one activity to another at frequent intervals, and subject to many interruptions (phone calls, people 'dropping in', ad hoc discussions, etc.). There is no contradiction here between theory and reality. Rather, it is the difference between management activities viewed in the abstract and carried out in practice.

Probably the best known and most influential study in this area is by Henry Mintzberg who lists[13] a number of propositions about the characteristics of managerial work, such as

- Because of the open-ended nature of his job, the manager feels compelled to perform a great quantity of work at an unrelenting pace. Little free time is available and breaks are rare.
- The activities of the manager are characterised by brevity, variety and fragmentation. The lack of pattern, with the trivial interspersed with the consequential, requires that the manager shift moods quickly and frequently.
- The manager actually appears to prefer brevity and inter-ruption in his work. He becomes conditioned by his work-load. Superficiality is an occupational hazard of the manager's job.
- The manager gravitates to the more active elements of his work – the current, the specific, the well-defined, the non-routine activities. The pressure of the job does not encourage the development of a planner, but of an adaptive information manipulator who works in a stimulus-response environment and who favours live action.
- Verbal and written contacts are the manager's work and his prime tools are five media – mail, telephone, unscheduled meetings, scheduled meetings, and tour. The manager clearly

favours the three verbal media, (i.e. phone, discussion, meetings) spending most of his time in verbal contact.

● The manager's job reflects a blend of duties and rights. Although superficial study of managers' activities suggests that they often control little of what they do, closer analysis suggests that the manager can exert self control in two important ways. The manager is responsible for many initial commitments, which then lock him into a set of ongoing activities; and the manager can take advantage of his obligations by extracting information, by exercising his leadership, and in many other ways.

(Adaptation of pp.51 – 3 from *The nature of managerial work* by Henry Mintzberg. Copyright © 1973 by Henry Mintzberg. Reprinted by permission of Harper & Row, Publishers, Inc.)

Comparing Mintzberg's propositions with Lawrence's definition gives some clues to the pressure – the 'executive stress' – of a manager's job. Personality factors are clearly important, but it would seem, in general, that managers are drawn to action rather than reflection, to verbal communication rather than more considered documentation, to a day of brief encounters characterized by variety and fragmentation with the ever-present danger of giving issues – and people – only superficial treatment. Yet, in the midst of this busy-ness (as itemized by Mintzberg), the manager must try to remain effective (in terms of the activities identified in Lawrence's definition). Drucker stresses the 'integrative' function of management – integrating parts of the organization into a coherent whole, and bringing together immediate and future considerations. He describes graphically[14] the manager's need to move towards longer-term goals while, at the same time, getting through the day's work. 'He must, so to speak, keep his nose to the grindstone while lifting his eyes to the hills – which is quite an a acrobatic feat.' This pressure can be compounded by the fact that the manager's job is open-ended. It is often up to the individual manager to decide how much time is to be spent working or thinking about work; or how the working day is to be organized.

Levels of management
The concept of 'executive stress', Mintzberg's propositions, and

the elements in Lawrence's definition do not apply only to 'senior' management – or to 'middle management' operating within a large organizational system. Managers at lower levels in the organizational hierarchy also have the challenge of balancing day-to-day busy work and longer-term goals, and often have a role to play in relation to one or more of the elements in Lawrence's definition

- involvement in the 'management cycle' (planning, organizing, directing, controlling);
- involvement in the 'people dimension' (communicating, motivating, maintaining commitment; 'developing people'; supervising);
- involvement in the decision-making and problem-solving processes.

This is particularly true of library work. The organizational structure of library systems is characterized by decentralization into small units with, in many cases, considerable autonomy in the way each unit organizes day-to-day activities. This involves newly-qualified librarians, at an early stage of their careers, in management-level responsibilities. In addition, many librarians find themselves working in 'one-person' libraries – small units in schools, colleges, commercial concerns, volunteer organizations – where one qualified member of staff is responsible for all aspects of the service.[15]

Three case studies illustrate the ways in which management can become an important aspect of an entry-level professional post.

- Imogen, Assistant Librarian in a public branch library: deputy to the Branch Librarian; day-to-day supervisory control of library assistants; responsible for the planning and implementation of 'outreach' services.
- Dorothy, Assistant Librarian in a specialist department of a university library: deputy to the department's Reader Services Librarian; day-to-day control of all circulation desk activities including supervision and training of library assistants; involvement in automation planning.
- Patrick, Librarian at a small community college: a 'one-person' library with Patrick responsible for all aspects of

library service within the college, including the library's budget.

In what ways, and to what extent, are these recently qualified professional librarians operating as managers? All are working not just with but *through* other people, Imogen and Dorothy supervising a team of library assistants and Patrick coordinating the mix of part-time, volunteer and student staffing which is typical of schools and colleges in the UK. In the human-relations areas of leadership and motivation each has a particular challenge: Patrick to maintain commitment in a largely volunteer workforce; Dorothy to train a new group of recently graduated library assistants each year; Imogen to develop new areas of service with a group of long-serving staff used to the old ways of working.

All have some responsibility for the efficient management of resources – not so much of money (although Patrick is accountable for a budget), but of staff time in order to provide an effective service. All are also involved in planning and decision-making, not just in relation to day-to-day operations, but also in matters of long-term strategic importance. Patrick is considering the implications for library service of changing teaching and assessment methods and also the possible library applications of information technology; Dorothy is helping to plan the implementation of an automated system; Imogen is shifting the emphasis of service away from the library building and into the local community. Each has responsibility (and thus accountability) for a particular area of work. Within the boundaries of that responsibility, each has authority to delegate tasks, to organize work-flow, and to use discretion and initiative. Each is also contributing to innovation; involved in planning, and implementing, future directions for their library service. Thus each has, within his or her job, the two core elements which emerge from Mintzberg's propositions and Lawrence's definition: the authority to exercise choice and discretion, with a certain 'open-ended-ness' to the job; and a 'development' dimension involving longer-term strategy as well as day-to-day operations.

One important point to make here, with reference to these examples, is that management, in libraries, is not just the province of professional staff. There is an unfortunately sharp division, in UK librarianship, between 'professionals' and 'non-professionals', the dividing line being successful completion of an approved course of study at a 'library school'. This is achieved either by full-time study or by part-time study over a period of some years and can be a difficult hurdle for many vocationally-talented library assistants to overcome. There is nothing in the UK at present which equates to the 'technician' or 'para-professional' grade of staff common in other countries. It is important to remember that library assistants form the 'front line' of service delivery and are thus crucial to the good management of customer relations. They are also, quite often, responsible for key processes within the core operations of library service, and are sometimes responsible for the day-to-day running of a service point. Senior Library Assistants have a vital role to play in team building – creating the good 'team spirit' that is necessary if a group is to work together effectively. There is a significant training need here, that must be recognized when constructing training and development programmes for library staff.

In libraries, as in other types of organization, there has been a move in recent years to 'flatten' hierarchies, devolve responsibility and authority downwards, improve communications upwards, and widen participation in decision-making. Clearly, different levels of staff will be involved in different aspects of management activity. The further 'up the ladder', the more time will be spent on 'managerial' rather than 'technical/professional' functions, the more concern will be for strategic rather than operational issues, the more focus will be on the five-year horizon rather than next week's timesheet. Even so, the logical extension of the flattened-hierarchy concept is that, where possible and appropriate, library assistants should be involved in the management process as participants and not just as victims.

At what level, then, does one become a 'manager'? It can be argued, of course, that the first level is management of self. We each have some control over the way in which we use our time – training in effective time management is becoming big business – and we certainly have control over the *effort* which we invest in an activity. This is particularly true in any form of service activity, like a library, where the quality of a customer's experience is determined largely by the attitude of the staff. Even the most mundane of library jobs – shelving and tidying, staffing the circulation desk – can be done well or badly: with a care for order and a cheerful smile; or with sloppiness and a glum look. Additionally, we are each responsible for our own personal integrity. Drucker stresses[16] the importance of integrity in management – the importance of consistency, of not 'playing favourites', of being firm but fair. Integrity and honesty are vital to good interpersonal relations and are thus crucial to the effectiveness of any group of people working together.

However, in organizational terms, management usually begins with responsibility – when an individual is given delegated authority (and accountability) for a particular function within the organization. The nature of this responsibility will differ on different hierarchical levels. At a 'junior' managerial level, responsibility is primarily operational – organizing a particular aspect of the service – with the manager directly involved in doing the work for which he or she is responsible. There is, in the day's work, a mix of managerial activity and technical/professional activity (that is, the exercise of librarianship skills: cataloguing, online searching, reference enquiry work, reader advice work, etc.). At senior level, responsibility is more to do with planning and strategy; more concerned with organizing and supporting the technical/professional work which others will do.

Two other dimensions can be added to help define the different levels of management activity. One is the 'integrative' function of coordinating different elements within the organization and harmonizing the two time dimensions of present activities and future planning. Clearly, there is more of this 'integrative' activity at higher levels of the management hierarchy. The second is the concept of choice. This has been applied to management work by Rosemary Stewart who has developed a framework[17] based on three categories: demands, constraints, and choices. *Constraints* are the internal and external factors which limit what a job-holder *can* do. *Demands* are those things which the job-holder *must* do. *Choices* are the activities which the job-holder can, but does not have to, do. Choices represent the opportunities within a job for one person to do different things from another and to do them in different ways.

There is a link, here, with Mintzberg's propositions regarding the open-ended-ness and element of discretion in a manager's job. Stewart provides a useful framework to apply to library work. It highlights, for example, the difference between the work pattern of a librarian in a branch library where provision is building-based and highly routinized in response to heavy demand for traditional lending; and the work pattern of someone on the same grade in a public library system which has evolved a community-oriented, outreach-based, 'team' approach to service. On the one hand, constraints and demands may leave little room for choice; on the other, there is wide scope for choice and discretion within the overall framework of the team's objectives for the service.

Stewart's model illustrates an important point about library work. It is not necessarily the case that there is more choice and less demand/constraint as one rises through the hierarchical levels; a job in the front line of service delivery may have more scope for choice than a job further up the hierarchy which is more closely concerned with the enabling bureaucracies of the organization. Linked to this – and to Mintzberg's point about a manager's control over his or her own work – is the relative autonomy which many librarians enjoy. There is considerable scope (in one-person libraries, public branch libraries, academic subject or site libraries) for an individual at a relatively early career stage to exercise choice and discretion in defining the content of a job and the way in which it is done.

Structure of the book
The structure of this book follows, to a large extent, the classic management cycle of planning, organizing/directing, and control. The approach to these management functions is conditioned by the library perspective and also by the general points raised in this introduction.

The challenge of change and the importance of a 'customer first' approach have particular relevance for the planning process. What is the value of forward planning in a time of discontinuous change? How can the planning of library service incorporate a 'marketing' approach, building in the demands, wants and needs of the customer community? The contrast between management theory and the reality of managing is also highlighted by the planning process. In theory decision-making is based on rationality; the logical and informed assessment of options. In practice it is often based on intuition, information which is to hand (but possibly incomplete), and a strong element of institutional and personal politics. Power politics and the force of personality may not always be rational, but they are massively influential in most organizations.

Organizing and directing recognizes the complex 'psychological contract' between people and organizations; and also the important interaction between organizations and their external environments. Theories of the 'adaptive' organization and the organization as organism are linked to the 'people dimension' and strategies for achieving 'excellence' in terms of individual and organizational performance. The importance of organizational 'culture' is stressed; as is the need to strike a balance between creativity and innovation on the one hand, and stability and control on the other.

The concept of control raises the issue of accountability and the importance of feedback systems to monitor performance. A particular challenge for libraries, here, is to build indicators of 'quality' and 'value' into these feedback systems.

Two particularly powerful external forces for change are technology and economics, and both are having a profound impact on the thinking of library managers. Technology can alter, for example

- objectives and strategies; the nature of service.
- operational structures; the ways in which service is delivered.
- productivity and the 'people dimension'; the work done by library staff.
- feedback systems; mechanisms for management information and decision support.

Economics condition the resource environment in which libraries operate. Library managers exercise budget control, and are also having to develop new areas of financial expertise. The move to greater accountability brings with it a requirement to define costs and link income more closely to performance.

Chapters on planning, organization, staff, technology, quality control, and financial management are followed by a final chapter which summarizes key points from the perspective of managing change.

The organization of the future
Library management has relevance for a wider audience than,

simply, librarians. Much early management theory was based on the study of private-sector corporations in the manufacturing/production industries. However, increasingly, management theorists and consultants are concerned with organizations which are not 'business' or 'product' based.

Libraries are service organizations. They are thus important in the context of a general shift from a manufacturing/production-based economy to an economy based on service industries. For example, a major concern in service industries is the quality of interaction between staff and customer – how to ensure excellence at the front line of service delivery. This is a challenge of particular pertinence to library managers.

Libraries are (usually) not-for-profit organizations. As such they illustrate the challenge to build accountability and enterprise into organizations where there is, traditionally, no direct relationship between income/expenditure and performance. How is accountability to the governing framework of resource-providers weighed against responsibility to the customer community? How can 'successful' performance be measured? How can a culture of market-led innovation be developed within a tradition of supply-led provision? How can enterprise replace bureaucratic inertia? Is it possible to find synergy between the 'service' ethic and the 'business' approach?

Libraries employ a professional, knowledge-based workforce. Libraries thus reflect two crucial workforce issues: the changing nature of employment in the 'post-industrial' society with increasing numbers of people working with knowledge/information as their raw material; and the debate over the nature and desirability of professionalism.

Peter Drucker, in *Innovation and entrepreneurship*, writes[18] of the need for management to reconsider issues of deployment, control and motivation in relation to the rise of the 'knowledge worker'. The nature of the relationship between organizational goals and personal/professional goals is different when the individual has expertise and a measure of autonomy. This has to be reflected in organizational structures, management styles, and decision-making processes. Drucker and others have suggested that organizations will become structured less as centralized hierarchies and more as decentralized 'federations' of relatively autonomous units. This is characteristic of the structure – if not always of the traditional management style – of large library systems.

Two further issues of general management concern have particular pertinence for library managers. One is equality of opportunity and the position of women within the workforce. The other is the challenge of managing new technology on strategic, operational and behavioural levels.

The image of libraries is a negative one – a service which is worthy, but dull. In fact, managing library service encompasses many of the exciting and crucial challenges facing management today.

It is important that library managers rise to these challenges. Professional librarians in line management jobs sometimes focus only on the *librarianship* aspect of their job; and ignore or reject their *management* role. In some library organizations, traditional structures and styles – and the attitudes and approaches of senior staff – reinforce this perspective. However, the world is changing. Increased accountability and a move to decentralized 'cost-centre' decision-making means that librarians must face up to their dual role: as professionally skilled librarians; and as managers with a responsibility to invest resources efficiently and effectively in order to achieve results. If librarians do not show the attitudes and aptitudes required to manage library service, then non-librarian managers will be brought in to do the job.

References

1 Nick Moore and Elaine Kempson, *Financing development: the use of external funds by public libraries*, British Library Research and Development Report number 5876, Bath, Parker Moore, 1986.
2 Thomas J. Peters and Robert H. Waterman, *In search of excellence: lessons from America's best-run companies*, New York, Harper & Row, 1982.
3 *Report by the Minister for the Arts on library and information matters during 1982* (HC 332), HMSO, 1988. Para. 15.
4 *Ibid.*, para. 16.
5 *Financing our public library service: four subjects for debate* (Cm 324), HMSO, 1988. Para 4.3.
6 See for example, Robert R. McClarren, 'Improving access through multitype library networking' in Alphonse F. Trezza (ed.), *Public libraries and the challenges of the next two decades*, Littleton, Colorado, Libraries Unlimited Inc., 1985.

7 See *The future development of libraries and information services: progress through planning and partnership*, Library Information Series number 14, HMSO, 1986.

8 See *Joint enterprise: roles and relationships of the public and private sectors in the provision of library and information services*, Library Information Series number 16, HMSO, 1987. In the USA, the concept of joint ventures between public and private sectors has been put forward by a number of commentators; for example, Linda Crismond, 'The future of public library service' in *Library journal*, **111**, (November 15, 1986), pp.42 – 9.

9 Peter Lawrence, *Invitation to management*, Oxford, Blackwell, 1986, pp.2 – 3.

10 Charles B. Handy, *Understanding organizations*, Harmondsworth, Penguin, 3rd edition, 1985, p.42.

11 Peter Drucker, *The practice of management*, Heinemann, 1955, pp.337 – 8.

12 See Peter Lawrence, *Management in action*, Routledge and Kegan Paul, 1984.

13 Henry Mintzberg, *The nature of managerial work*, New York, Harper and Row, 1973, pp.51 – 3. The list in the text is an edited selection of Mintzberg's full list of propositions.

14 Drucker, *The practice of management*, p.336.

15 See Guy St. Clair and Joan Williamson, *Managing the one-person library*, Butterworth, 1986.

16 Drucker, *The practice of management*, p.155.

17 Rosemary Stewart, *Choices for the manager: a guide to managerial work and behaviour*, McGraw-Hill, 1982, pp.2 – 3.

18 Peter Drucker, *Innovation and entrepreneurship: practice and principles*, Pan/Heinemann, 1986.

2 The planning process

Introduction

In the planning process the library manager has to take account of three 'constituencies' of people – the library staff, the customer community, and the governing framework for the library service. Issues to do with the library staff are discussed in Chapters Three and Four. In this chapter, the focus is on planning in relation to the other two constituencies.

The governing framework will always have a major impact on the planning process because the library manager's delegated authority comes from that framework. At any managerial level, the organization's hierarchical structure of delegation and accountability (i.e. the reporting structure), has to be taken into account and built into the planning mechansim. It is not part of the purpose of this book to describe in detail the governing framework for library services but, in general terms, the basic model is the same for most libraries:

- a hierarchical structure within the library system (from library assistant to chief librarian) which affects the internal processes of planning and implementation.
- a larger hierarchical structure which sets the library into the context of the 'parent' organization of which it is a part and defines the governing framework within that organization.
- the wider framework of policy and legislation determined by national government.

There are exceptions – one-person libraries rarely have a formal hierarchy within the library system, and national libraries are rarely set into a larger organizational context. But, on the whole, this three-tier model (library, organizational structure, government context) holds good. The structure and internal mechanisms of the parent organization have a direct impact on library planning in that they define how policy directions and resource allocations are decided. The government context too can have a significant impact through legislation. For example, an agenda of current legislative issues which could be incorporated into a library service's strategic thinking might include

- reform of the law on intellectual property (i.e. copyright);
- data protection;
- freedom of access to information (or, in the UK, a possible redefinition of the 'official secrets' act);
- implications for information provision of broadcasting legislation (e.g. satellite provision, community radio, community cable); and of telecommunications legislation.

In addition to these general issues related to information, specific areas of legislation are having a major impact on library planning in particular sectors. For example, current UK legislation is affecting the structure and funding of higher education, and the curriculum and assessment methods used in schools; and, in due course, the government's consultative paper, *Financing our public library service: four subjects for debate*, may lead to new or revised legislation.

The governing framework has to be taken into account when planning because that framework controls matters of policy and resourcing within the organization. However, a market-led approach (responding to and anticipating the demands, wants and needs of customers) suggests that the customer community should also be built into the planning process.

In some cases the customer community overlaps with the governing framework, especially when the library operates in a 'closed' environment such as an academic institution or business corporation; in these cases the customer community is made up of people who are themselves part of the organizational structure. For example, the governing framework of an academic institution in which policy and resource issues are determined (governing body, academic board, faculty boards, etc.) is made up, largely, of people – academic staff, administrative staff, student representatives – who might also be library customers.

This is not the case with public libraries where the community served may have (notional) geographic boundaries, but is much more 'open' in terms of potential customers. However, there is still overlap in that the governing framework (in the UK, the local Council committee; in the USA, the Board of Trustees) is made up of representatives elected by the local people who form a major part of the customer community. In the USA, a further link between libraries and their customer communities is provided by the influential 'Friends of the library' movement. 'Friends' do not determine policy or control finance – these are the responsibilities of Trustees – but successful Friends groups work in close partnership with Trustees, and so contribute to the common goal of meeting local need.[1]

Building the customer community into the planning process raises two difficult issues. First, how is it possible to identify the needs and wants – as opposed to explicit articulated demands – of customers? Second, how can the conflict be reconciled when there is discrepancy between policy (relating to customer service) and resourcing (as determined by the governing framework)? The first question can be answered, in part, by adopting a 'marketing approach' or 'customer focus' to planning. The second requires library managers to engage in the 'political' process of making choices and allocating resources.

Definition and value

Planning involves action taken in the present with regard to the future. This integration of present and future suggests that planning involves an element of forecasting/anticipation. It also involves a consideration of both *ends* (outcomes in the future) and *means* (ways of bringing about those outcomes). In fact, there are five elements to be considered in any plan:

- *Ends* – what are the goals and objectives; the desired outcomes?
- *Means* – what policies, programmes, procedures and practices are to be used?
- *Resources* – what types and amounts of resources are required, how are these to be generated or acquired, and how are they to be allocated to activities?
- *Implementation* – what decision-making procedures are needed

27

and how are these to be organized?

- *Control* – what will be the 'control' procedure for anticipating or detecting errors in, or failures of, the plan and for preventing or correcting them on a continuing basis?

An important element implicit in these considerations is the concept of a timescale. If a plan sets out the strategies and stages for achieving a set of desired future outcomes then, clearly, it should include some indication of the length of time involved at each stage. This then provides a means of monitoring progress (is the plan running 'to schedule'?) and so contributes to the 'control' procedure.

Three further points need to be made to complete the definition. The most important is that planning is a continuous and dynamic process. An important product of that process is the planning document[2] – important because it

- formalizes the work done during the planning process;
- informs staff (and customers) of plans;
- serves as a reference source for future decision-making.

But the planning document is only an interim statement; a staging-post in a continuous process. No plan is final – it must always be capable of adjustment and refinement to meet changing circumstances. In addition, the *process* of planning has considerable value for those involved, irrespective of the product – the plan – which results.

The second point is that planning involves coordination. Planning any event – a holiday, a programme of summertime children's activities, an arts festival, the implementation of an automated circulation system – involves a multiplicity of decisions, bringing together a number of disparate elements. It is thus an important part of the 'integrative' function of management.

Thirdly, planning has been defined as the process of turning objectives into actions – indeed 'taking action' has been described as 'one of the most exciting steps in the planning process'.[3] This stresses the link between *ends* and *means*. By taking an objective – or set of objectives – as the starting point, the process of planning gives a sense of purpose and direction to an organization.

We have already seen that organizations – including libraries – are subject to strong external forces for change. In a time of change it is particularly important to keep a clear focus on *ends* and *means*.

Organizations are sometimes described as 'open systems', interacting with and adapting to their environment. This interaction can be of two types – pro-active, or re-active. The pro-active organization knows where it is going, operates a strong and continuous process of planning, is prepared for change, and so can adapt while maintaining a sense of direction. The re-active organization spends little time on forward planning, does not foresee problems and issues which arise as a result of changing circumstances, and thus either loses a sense of direction and begins to 'drift', or expends much energy in hasty, last-minute decision-making; or does both. A major value of planning is that it can help an organization avoid these two failings which can have a critical impact on performance and morale. The cycle of 'crisis management' (see Figure 4) leads to stress and poor decision-making. The tendency of organizations to lose direction and drift means also a tendency to lose dynamism and develop a high degree of bureaucratic inertia. The planning process provides management with a tool to combat inertia and replace reaction with a forward-thinking, pro-active approach.

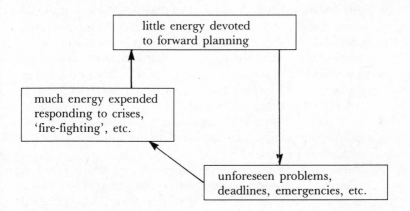

Figure 4: The cycle of 'crisis' management

The process of arriving at an agreed (and documented) set of objectives and strategies has a number of values in addition to the overall advantages of providing a sense of direction and helping the organization adapt, pro-actively, to change.

- It generates rigorous thinking about purpose, policy and resources, crystallizing points of agreement and clarifying areas of dispute, confusion or vagueness. Planning public library service, for example, can lead to a more stringent and precise definition of the purpose of that service.
- It focusses attention on key issues by making them explicit and documented. For example, many organizations now have documented plans regarding an 'equal opportunities' policy in order to keep under active scrutiny the balance of gender and ethnicity in the workforce.
- It promotes systematic thinking about the future, extending time horizons and building a 'development' dimension into jobs.
- It creates useful information 'networks' within the organization to supplement other channels of communication and feedback.
- Participation in the planning process builds consensus and commitment. If staff are involved in the development of a policy or the planning for an event, they will feel some 'ownership' of that policy or event; feel that they have a personal stake in it. Thus they are likely to be strongly motivated towards ensuring its success. If a particular plan, or policy, or set of objectives and strategies is agreed by the governing framework then implicit in that support is a commitment to provide the resources which might be necessary in order to achieve what has been agreed.
- It helps towards the identification of 'success factors' – indicators which can be used to demonstrate the value and success of a service.
- If the planning process sets realistic targets which are then achieved it can lead to improved morale. One of the classic catchphrases[4] of 'people' management is 'People who feel good about themselves produce good results'.

People 'feel good about themselves' when they have a sense of achievement. The planning process – linked to good systems of feedback and appraisal – can provide this.

Of course, there are potential disadvantages too. Planning takes time and effort – and so is sometimes seen either as too costly or as having a tendency to delay decision-making and action. It is true that organizations sometimes 'set up a working party' in order to defer, delay or dodge the need to make a decision. A further disadvantage is that planning – or rather, the existence of a plan – can inhibit innovation and initiative. New ideas have to be fed into the 'planning cycle' or built into the 'corporate plan' before they can be acted on.

This conservatism – the use of planning to reduce uncertainty and increase conformity – is, as Charles Handy points out,[5] inappropriate when change is discontinuous and the environment unpredictable. Handy suggests that, in such a situation, organizations need to adopt an approach of experimentation akin to 'systematic gambling'. Security is sought in variety and collaboration with successes reinforced and failures discarded.

The experimental approach requires an organizational culture which stimulates innovation, supports individual initiative and accepts risk-taking. Thus the planning process does not become a straitjacket but provides a structured framework within which initiative can flourish. This co-existence of strong central direction and maximum individual autonomy gives what Peters and Waterman describe[6] as 'simultaneous loose-tight properties' to an organization. This seems a particularly useful model to apply to any decentralized organization which has operating units distributed over a wide geographic area – such as a public library system, or an academic library system which operates through a number of different sites or specialist departments.

However, it is important that experimentation and local autonomy are conditioned by a clear consensus view of the organization's purpose and direction. This lies behind another of the catchphrases to come out of *In search of excellence* – the idea that successful organizations 'stick to the knitting'; that is, they define carefully the business they are in, and stick to it. Niccolo Machiavelli, who is often quoted on the subject of change, noted that any organization needs regular 'reformation' to keep it fresh, alert, and relevant; and that, in successful organizations, that process of reformation involves 'a return to first principles'.[7]

Without a framework of 'first principles' – of agreed purpose and direction – an experimental approach can lead to incoherent and fragmented development influenced by short-term fashions and bandwagons. The 'knitting' becomes unravelled.

Planning, then, is of great importance at a time of change. It has even greater importance at a time when resources are constrained and it is imperative that organizations set priorities and review strategies in order to deploy those limited resources as efficiently and effectively as possible. For these reasons there is, at present, a strong emphasis on planning within librarianship in both the UK and the USA. *Advancing with knowledge: the British Library strategic plan, 1985 – 1990* – the first such plan produced by the British Library – focusses on precisely these reasons in its introduction:[8]

> The British Library thought it timely to review the whole range of its policies and set out a clear programme for the future. The Library's Strategic Plan is the result of this process . . . In developing its first Strategic Plan the Library has directed attention towards clarifying priorities, assessing users needs and exploring the scope and importance of developing new services, working closely and flexibly with others in the library and information industry so as to get the greatest benefit from the available resources.

The Library and Information Services Council (LISC), supported by the Office of Arts and Libraries (OAL) and the Minister for the Arts, is promoting[9] the concept of 'library and information plans' (LIPs):

> The library and information plan concept is of a five year management plan, drawn up by a local authority responsible for library services under the Public Libraries and Museums Act 1964. All the library and information services in the area (the public library, academic libraries and other library and information services in the public sector, as well as the industrial, commercial, professional and other library and information services in the private sector) would review what they currently provided and what they wanted to achieve. With this as a base line, they would agree how they could, in their own individual interests, contract with each other to make the

best use of the resources in the area. All would negotiate to get what they wanted, to supply what they wished, free or at a charge, for the benefit of their users.

The rationale behind this concept is, again, to maximize use of resources: 'Library and information services now need, not merely to supplement informal cooperation by more deliberately planned relationships, but to contract together within a library and information plan to provide services which make the maximum possible use of resources'.

The way that Library and Information Plans are beginning to work in practice emphasizes that planning is a dynamic and continuing process, rather than being concerned to produce a fixed and static 'plan'. Although beginning with a five-year time-frame, in practice the LIP 'rolls forward' with a development plan for the next three years, reviewed annually. This process of an annual policy planning cycle setting objectives which are firmly targetted (for the first year), indicative (for the second year) and aspirational (for the third year) is becoming a feature of good management practice in all types of organizations.

In both the UK and the USA there has been a move – certainly in public libraries – away from the concept of national standards and towards the development of a planning framework which can be adapted and used by individual library services. This work is particularly well advanced in the USA where the Public Library Association (a division of the American Library Association) has produced extensive and useful documentation on the processes of planning, 'role setting' (that is, determining priorities for service), and performance evaluation.[10] As the manual on *Planning and role-setting for public libraries* (prepared as part of the Public Library Development Program notes:[11] 'No library can fulfil all roles with excellence, so each library must focus its resources on a *limited* number of roles.' The manual offers eight roles which are (it admits) generalized and overlapping, but which provide a useful starting point for a public library attempting to define its purpose and priorities.

The PLA emphasizes that planning, if done thoroughly, is both radical and political: radical because it involves reappraisal, risk-taking, and a re-examination of the library's role in relation to its customer community; political because it requires managers to make choices between competing priorities and seek out resources in order to put those decisions into action:[12]

> Planning inevitably means change. The library is re-examining itself and questioning its assumptions about its community and its priorities for service. The library and its staff have to be willing to stand back and ask themselves whether they are providing the most-needed services in the most effective way possible. They must look forward to the future needs of their community, not just backward to the way that they have traditionally served their users.

> Planning is risk-taking. It requires hard decisions about fundamental aspects of the library in the community ... Planning is radical, in the most basic sense of the term: going back to the root of the matter. The planning group begins by defining the role of the library in its community. The library's goals, objectives, and strategies are rooted in this decision.

> Planning is also political ... The Board [Council, etc.] represents the interests of the community in library policy-making; it is also the library's liaison with the political process. The planning process itself is inevitably political, involving as it does the weighing of the needs of various interest groups. Furthermore, the results of the planning process will provide input into the budget process, as the library seeks the funding to accomplish its plan.

In the USA, like the UK, the library world is one of diversity and plurality. In different libraries and regions there will be differences in the services being planned. But in all types of library and on both sides of the Atlantic, there is a common recognition of the centrality of the planning *process*.

Planning and decision-making
Given that planning is often described as decision-making with regard to the future, it is not surprising that there is considerable overlap, in management literature, between theoretic studies of the planning process and those focussing on the decision-making process. Both activities involve all or most of the following four elements

34

- choice (between alternatives);
- risk (of choosing what might turn out to be a 'wrong' option);
- other people (either involved in the planning/decision-making process itself; or affected by the results of that process; or both);
- complexity (solving multidimensional problems; coordinating multiple decisions).

Both activities take time. Planning is – or should be – a continuous process, and the same can be true of decision-making.

There is, of course, a difference between decisions in the arena of policy-making (strategic, long-term) and those concerned with problem-solving (operational, short-term). The former are likely to be pro-active, considered, and the result of an incremental and collective process – building up evidence, opinions and consensus until the decision emerges. This type of decision-making is indistinguishable from the concept of planning. The latter are more likely to be re-active, taken quickly by an individual after a relatively brief period of information-gathering and consultation. However, even these 'snap' decisions are influenced by their context, which has built up over time. Decisions which appear to be re-active, immediate, and individualistic are informed (either consciously or unconsciously) by the accumulated experience of the decision-maker and the corporate heritage and culture of the organization. This explains why, for a manager newly arrived in an organization, it is sometimes more difficult to make rapid problem-solving decisions than to plan policy and strategy: the rapid decision has to be taken without full knowledge of the organization's heritage and culture; policy-making can incorporate such considerations.

The important point is that decisions, like plans, are the result of a process; and that the process itself is as important as the outcome. For this reason, many management writers prefer to use the term 'decision-*making*' rather than 'decision-*taking*'. The process can be analysed in terms of nine stages. In practice, these stages are sometimes separate and distinguishable (for example, within the formal 'policy planning' cycle of an organization) and sometimes telescoped and compressed into a brief ad hoc discussion. But all are – or should be – present.

- Awareness: getting the matter 'onto the agenda' – recognizing that there is a need for thought and action.
- Analysis: diagnosing or defining the issue to be addressed. What exactly is the nature of the 'problem' to be solved? What are the initial premises and assumptions on which the policy is to be based? What are the objectives?
- Investigation. Good decision-making requires information, and this is the stage at which the information is gathered. As well as bringing together objective and documented information, this can involve verbal consultation both inside and outside the organization; and is thus the point at which knowledge of the corporate heritage and culture can be built in to the process (unless this has already been identified as part of the problem).
- Alternatives: analysis and investigation come together and the various options for action are identified. An important part of this stage is creative thinking. An organizational culture which encourages participation, imagination and the free flow of ideas is likely to come up with a greater range of possible options and solutions – although some of the more 'creative' suggestions may need to be treated with due caution.
- Evaluation. Drucker[13] suggests four criteria for evaluating options and deciding on the best alternative:

  - risk in relation to expected return.
  - effort required.
  - timing (is dramatic change desirable, or is a gradual approach more suitable?)
  - availability of resources, especially of people.

- Decision. The choice is made and the chosen option is converted into a proposal for action.
- Communication.
- Implementation.
- Monitoring/review.

These final three stages are not the subject of this chapter but they must not be forgotten. Once a decision is made it is important that it be communicated, implemented and the effects monitored. Strategies for these three processes need to be considered carefully at the time that the decision is made.

The distinction between policy planning and problem-solving has already been made – although it is, more accurately, a continuum rather than a clear distinction with considered policy-making at one end and 'snap' decision-making at the other. A similar distinction needs to be made regarding different types of plans. These are basically of three types:

- Strategic plans, converting the basic goals and objectives of the organization into actions. Included here are: decisions regarding long-term strategic issues; operational plans to put strategies into effect and 'get the job done'; contingency plans to anticipate possible change (for example, change in the level or nature of funding for an organization or department); tactical plans focussing on the best way to approach a particular situation. An increasingly important category of strategic plan is the 'business plan' by which expected progress over time is set against target objectives for income and expenditure so that the likely financial performance and long-term viability of the project can be assessed. When bidding for 'pump-priming' funds to get a new initiative off the ground, libraries are often asked to provide a business plan to show how the initiative will be resourced and sustained once the initial funding period is over.
- Standing plans, dealing with matters of agreed policy (for example, on purchasing or equal opportunities) or procedure (for example, grievance or disciplinary procedures); or with rules and regulations (for example, those which apply when a customer borrows a library book). The existence of standing plans makes possible an element of 'programmed' decision-making where the facts fit into an existing agreed framework which largely predetermines the decision.
- Single-use plans, dealing with one-off projects and pro-grammes. These can range from major organization-wide considerations (for example, library automation or the development of a staff training programme) to relatively small-scale single events such as a Saturday morning 'children's activity' session in a neighbourhood branch library.

Different levels of the management hierarchy are involved in these types of plans – and in the policy-making/problem-solving continuum – in different ways and with different perspectives. Senior management will take the long-term (say two to five years) view and focus on strategic issues. Middle management will be concerned with the interaction between strategic and operational issues and will take a mid-term view (say three months to three years). Junior management, or 'line' managers responsible for a particular function within the organization, will be concerned with operational issues in the short term (day, week, month).

Library automation can be used as a good example of this. The senior management team (in consultation – ideally – with staff, customers and the governing framework) makes the strategic decisions: what is to be automated, how is it to be done, when is it to be done? History would suggest, for example, that an early candidate for automation would be the circulation control system. Middle management – those managers in charge of individual sites or departments – interprets the strategic objectives in terms of the operational considerations of that particular service unit: what needs to be done in order to prepare for implementation? If the circulation system is to be automated, how can this best be fitted in to the normal pattern of work with least disruption of the service? Where will the equipment be sited and how will this affect the look and layout of the service point? When and how will the installation (for example, of cabling) take place? What training needs do the staff have and how can these best be met? Is there a need to prepare the stock (for example, by affixing bar-coded labels) for use with the new system? The junior line managers will then be charged with putting into action various of these operational considerations – planning the training programme, for example, or organizing the bar-coding of stock.

This example illustrates a number of key points. First, the level of uncertainty – the dimension of the indeterminate – is greater in decisions taken at senior levels in the hierarchy. The pressure at this level is created by the risk factor. Second, when strategic decisions have been taken, there is a considerable amount of work to be done in order to implement them effectively. Much of this work falls on middle management and the pressure at this level is created by the need to reconcile strategic objectives and operational requirements. Third, there is a need for dialogue between the different hierarchical levels. For junior management, the pressure is created by the need to get the job done. But it may be that decisions made further 'up the line' have not taken full account of the operational realities on the 'shop floor', so that junior management is faced with a task, or a timescale, which is unrealistic. The organizational culture should be such that the junior manager feels able to put forward alternative suggestions based on a 'shop floor' perspective – so that the processes of communication and decision-making in the organization have a 'bottom-up' as well as a 'top-down' dynamic. Involving all relevant staff in the planning process means that:

- 'shop floor' considerations will be taken into account;
- staff will feel that they have a 'stake' in – and thus a commitment to – the decisions made;
- staff gain a sense of involvement which can have a positive effect on morale and motivation, and so on the quality of customer service.

Planning and decision-making are human processes. There is a place for quantitative methods, but the statistical data derived from clipboard, calculator and computer – although important and sometimes underdeveloped in library management – is only one dimension of a multifaceted complex of considerations.

One consequence of the human dimension is that decision-making is not always an entirely rational process. Rather than the cold application of logic in evaluating options and deciding upon a course of action, there is often an element of intuition or conviction which determines the eventual outcome. Intuition and conviction – or, 'judgements based on experience' – are necessary because decisions are rarely taken with the benefit of comprehensive knowledge regarding alternatives and outcomes. Rather, they are made on the basis of 'limited' rationality – limited by the time and energy available for investigation and analysis.

Planning and decision-making, then, illustrate the difference, common in all areas of management, between theory and practice. The theory suggests a staged process which is logical and scientific. But practice indicates that there are a number of barriers impeding a 'scientific' approach

- uncertainty regarding potential outcomes;

- lack of comprehensive information (including, in many organizations, poor management information systems of feedback and control);
- the human dimension of intuition and conviction;
- the compromises and adjustments often necessary to reconcile strategic objectives with operational reality, in terms of both 'shop floor' requirements and also the heritage and culture of the organization;
- the cost of the effort in time and energy;
- the quality of analytic and creative thought needed;
- the difficulty of finding opportunities for effective forward planning amidst the busy-work of day-to-day activities.

However, just as planning is important in order to create a well-directed, forward-thinking, pro-active organization, so too is firm decision-making. Indecision creates tension, vacillation and uncertainty. Managers at all levels need to have the courage and confidence to be decisive – as well as the open-ness and confidence to accept responsibility for errors of judgement and learn from mistakes. This requires an organizational culture which has a positive approach to decision-making, accepting that it involves a degree of risk, and is supportive of individuals by converting poor decisions into constructive learning and developmental experiences.

A political process
Because the process of planning and decision-making is a very human one it carries with it a strong 'political' dimension. This does not mean party politics as practised in government – although in the UK libraries are very much part of the political agenda as defined by government – but the 'office politics' or institutional politicking which goes on in any organization.

There is likely to be, in any decision-making process, an element of informal discussion and 'lobbying' in addition to formal meetings and consultations. Indeed, in the United States, lobbying on behalf of various interest groups has become big business. This informal but influential process is recognized in the commonplace assumption that *real* decision-making goes on 'behind the scenes' by a select group of power-brokers in 'smoke-filled rooms'. This is a key point in F. M. Cornford's classic *Microcosmographia academica*[14] which provides a splendidly wry look at university decision-making and describes deals being struck (or rather interests being 'squared') while the interested parties stroll in a seemingly casual but actually highly contrived way on the 'King's Parade'.

Every organization has, to a greater or lesser extent, a 'King's Parade' where the process of politicking – informing, influencing, lobbying, negotiating, discussing possible trade-offs – takes place outside the formal decision-making arenas. Roger Stoakley, Chief Librarian of Somerset, puts this[15] with judicious care:

> In local government, as in other organizations with a formal committee structure, a great deal of business is done behind the scenes. A chance conversation with a councillor in the street, over lunch, or at a social function might well clear up a misunderstanding in his own mind about our service or provide us with an opportunity to express a particular viewpoint.

In order to be a successful player in organizational decision-making – for example, to further the interests of the library against competing claims from other sections of the organization – it is necessary to locate the centres of power and gain access to them. The continuing success of the library depends on gaining and maintaining the support, commitment, and good will of opinion-makers amongst the customer community and within the governing framework. Patricia Breivik, for example, writing on the development of library instruction programmes in American schools, emphasizes the political dimension – the importance of winning support from influential people within the organization – if a new initiative is to become an established programme.[16] As John Cowley, erstwhile Head of Library Services at Middlesex Polytechnic, has written:[17] 'It is absolutely necessary for librarians to be part of the power structure of the institution.'

A necessary prerequisite of this, of course, is to *understand* the organization's power structure: the internal dynamics, encompassing the 'behind the scenes' dimension as well as the formal decision-making arenas. There are three aspects to this. First is the need – at senior management level – to be seen as having a broad corporate perspective not a narrowly-based interest only in those matters which impinge on library service. Second is the concept of 'boundary management' – recognizing the potential impact on the library service of external forces, and keeping a close watch on those key externalities. 'Boundary management' links to the idea of the organization as an open system, interacting with its environments – including the 'political' dimension of those environments – in a pro-active way. A major strategy for good boundary management is building up informal 'networks' of contacts; deliberately seeking to create cooperative relationships outside the confines of the library. These can be used simply as an information source – a means of 'keeping in touch' with the wider context; as defensive and preventative strategies to protect the library's interests; and as part of an entrepreneurial strategy of identifying and capitalizing on opportunities as they arise. Being 'in the right place at the right time' requires good boundary management.

The third aspect for librarians attempting to become part of the power structure of the parent organization is the need for political acumen – awareness and understanding not only of the formal power structure, but also of any underlying dynamics in terms of issues (the 'hidden agenda'), people (cliques and power groups), or processes (the 'King's Parade').

In all decision-making situations where the library service is in competition with other departments for limited resources – or where different interest-groups within the library service are vying with each other for priority – there will be a political dimension, and a trade-off between service aspirations, political considerations and resource constraints (see Figure 5). Andrew Pettigrew[18] describes decision-making not merely as a 'thought process' or a 'choice process', but as 'a political process that balances various power vectors'. Pettigrew defines 'political behaviour' as any action which seeks support for a claim on the organization's resources. Influencing the power-brokers and opinion-makers, generating support, and staking a claim for resources form the essence, then, of political activity in organizations.

At a time when there is pressure to do 'more with less' – an increasing number of service aspirations, but a decreasing level of available resourcing – there is a greater intensity of political activity. This pressure – for several years a major factor in British library management – is also being felt in the USA; Blodgett, for example, predicts a US fiscal future of restraint and creative

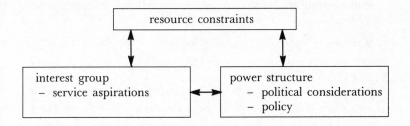

Figure 5: The trade-off between service aspirations and political considerations in a context of constrained resources

financing mechanisms which parallels the UK experience.[19] In this context library managers cannot afford to shy away from the process of politicking. If librarians are to be successful managers, they must take account of and engage with this dimension of institutional politics, both inside the library itself and also in the wider context of the parent organization.

A sense of direction
Fundamental to the planning process is the need to define, and express, purpose. Library purpose is defined by the needs of the customer community, and expressed through a set of aims and objectives. Getting closer to the customer community is a theme taken up later in the book. This section deals with the concept of objectives.

Setting objectives helps an organization maintain its sense of direction, and can help define the structure of the organization itself. For example, the academic library which has as its primary objective

> To provide books, documents and other media to support teaching and research within the institution.

is likely to have a structure which is different from the academic library which aims

> To make a positive contribution to the educational process within the institution by developing, in students and staff, the

43

information skills which are fundamental to independent learning.

Similarly, there will be a difference of structure between the public library with a set of objectives based on the provision of traditional lending and reference services from fixed and mobile service points and the public library which defines its aims in terms of outreach and community development. The ALA Public Library Development Program, for example, offers eight possible roles[20] for public libraries, as:

- centre for community activities.
- centre for community information.
- centre to support formal education.
- centre for independent learning.
- library of popular materials.
- door to learning for pre-school children.
- reference library.
- centre for research.

Each role has different implications for organizational structure and objectives; which is why combining roles – and reflecting those combinations in terms of priorities and structures – is a major challenge for public library managers.

As well as expressing purpose and helping to define structure, objectives also contribute to the process of 'control' – of monitoring and evaluating an organization's performance. As John Blagden, Librarian at the Cranfield Institute of Technology, writes:[21]

The management process essentially consists of setting objectives, evaluating alternative ways of reaching those objectives, selecting one alternative and then monitoring the success of the selected alternative in making progress towards that objective. Monitoring or evaluation is then an integral part of the management process simply and obviously because all libraries either implicitly or explicitly are attempting to achieve something.

Libraries are trying to 'achieve something'. A statement of objectives both defines what it is that the library is trying to

44

achieve, and also provides a statement of expressed intentions against which performance – progress towards achieving those intentions – can be assessed.

Creating a statement of objectives, like the overall planning process, is useful in building commitment within the governing framework of the organization to the nature and level of achievement at which the library service is aiming. The process of creating and reviewing such a statement – in consultation with key managers within the parent organization – should work to the library's benefit when the library manager puts in a bid for the resources needed in order to achieve those agreed objectives.

But what precisely is 'a statement of objectives'? And how do *objectives* differ from *aims* or *goals* or the *mission* of the organization – all terms which are commonly used in management literature? Whatever terms are used, the model is usually of a three-tier structure, defined here as *mission*, *aims* and *objectives*.

- *Mission*. This is a broad and aspirational statement of fundamental purpose. It defines the basic 'business' of the organization, often in a single sentence.
- *Aims*. These express long-term targets with each aim redefining the basic mission of the organization in terms of one particular area of work.
- *Objectives*. These convert each aim into a series of actions.

There is, then, a structured and logical relationship between each of the three tiers, and each has a particular value. The creation of a 'mission statement' is a rigorous intellectual exercise which concentrates the mind on the fundamentals of an organization's purpose and reason for existence. Creation of a set of aims arising out of that mission statement, each aim dealing with a particular area of work, ensures that all aspects of the organization are included and considered in terms of their contribution to that fundamental mission. Objectives then translate each aim into action – each objective expressing a single action which is achievable (within a given timescale) and measurable. Sometimes, each single action has to be broken down into a series of *sub-objectives* or individual *tasks*. Objectives are a statement of actions to be taken and targets to be achieved. They thus provide the link between planning – when the objectives and targets are set –

and control; when performance is measured against these targets.

A useful example of this tiered approach – although the terminology used is different – is the set of *Public library aims and objectives* produced, in the UK, by the Public Libraries Research Group.[22] This begins with an overall mission statement which is then interpreted in terms of four aims dealing with each of the four traditional aspects of public library purpose – education, information, culture, and leisure. Each of these aims is then translated into a set of objectives and activities. As well as this overall framework, each aspect of public library service (adult reference, adult lending, services to children, community information, etc., etc.) is given an aim and a consequent set of objectives and activities.

A similar three-tiered approach is used by the Public Library Association in America, although, again, the precise terminology differs:[23]

> While the library role statement points the directions in which the library will move, goals represent the ends towards which the library is striving over the planning period. They are not necessarily quantifiable statements. Objectives, however, are specific targets to be achieved during the planning period, measurable steps leading to the goals.

Objectives encompass all the specific, measurable activities which should lead to achieving the goal. Statements of objectives should include:

- the particular outcome desired;
- the measurement of achievement;
- the time frame.

An example (adapted from one given by the PLA) is: 'To increase the number of persons registered as library members to 50% of the total catchment population by 1992.'

The process of defining and expressing mission, aims and objectives can play a major part in the 'integrating' function of management – bringing all elements of the organization together into a coherent whole, and getting everyone and everything 'pulling in the same direction'. It is also a necessary foundation for the 'control' function of management – providing a set of expressed aspirations and intentions against which actual achievements can be compared.

The process also helps – by defining purpose and translating 'mission' into actions – in determining priorities. Resources are always finite and statements of what the library hopes and intends to achieve must always take account of that fact if they are to be realistic and useful. This is why the Public Library and Museums Act (1964), which requires local government in England and Wales to provide a 'comprehensive and efficient' public library service, is not particularly helpful; given finite resources, how can a 'comprehensive' service be achieved? This has been recognized both in the UK, where the Library and Information Services Council has noted:[24]

> Public libraries cannot literally provide the 'comprehensive service' which is asked of them by the Public Libraries and Museums Act 1964 and so they must in practice select the client groups to whose needs they will give priority in allocating their resources.

and in the USA, in the work on 'role setting' carried out by the Public Library Association. The PLA manual on *Planning and role setting*[25] accepts that public libraries cannot be all things to all people, and that choices have to be made.

Thus, locally set objectives – based on a local definition of roles and priorities, and expressed through locally agreed targets – become the basis of the planning/control cycle. There can be difficulties and dangers with this concept of 'management by objectives'.

- The amount of time and paperwork sometimes involved (if the result is a complex and time-consuming procedure of 'reporting back' on progress).
- A focus on the short-term and the quantifiable, at the expense of longer-term strategy and less tangible outcomes and achievements.
- Staff who feel threatened and inhibited by pressure to achieve particular objectives.

However, these problems can be tackled. The process of creating, implementing and reviewing a set of aims and objectives is done by consultation not by imposition. Success in effectively integrating all elements in the organization requires consensus about what the organization is trying to achieve. Feedback procedures are streamlined, focussing only on key 'performance indicators'. This subject will be discussed in Chapter 6.

The process always takes as its basic point of reference the 'first principles' – the core values and roles – on which the service is based. In this way short-term targets are set into the framework of long-term aspirations.

The process of defining mission, aims, and objectives can help to:

- create a liberating, rather than a repressive, framework for individual action.
- strengthen commitment to the values, roles, aspirations and strategies of the service through consultation and consensus-building.

Such a process is particularly appropriate for a service organization like a library where: resources are largely dependent on the continuing commitment of the parent organization and its governing framework; individual members of staff are constantly, and independently, interacting with customers; and professional staff are often given a high degree of discretion and autonomy.

The marketing approach
If the purpose of library service is defined by the needs of its customers, and the 'success' of that service is determined by the perceptions and preferences of those customers, then, clearly, the customer community needs to be built into the planning/evaluation process. It is this focus on customers that lies behind the 'marketing' approach to service planning.

Librarians sometimes feel uneasy with this concept: partly because the idea of 'marketing' has acquired commercial connotations; and partly, perhaps, because the concept of a market-led service – driven by customer need – contradicts the traditionally subordinate and dependent relationship of 'client' to 'professional'. In this traditional relationship, service is supply-led, determined by 'professional' expertise and judgement. However, there is consensus, at least in the literature (if not always the practice) of librarianship, that library service should be *community* or *user* or *client* orientated.

Successful companies understand and interact closely with their markets[26] and the principles of marketing apply as much to a service organization like a library as they do to a business corporation. In simple terms, the market-led approach to planning begins with the customer community which forms the 'marketplace' for that library's services. The market is researched, needs ('gaps in the market') are identified, and products (services) are developed to meet those market needs. This is in contrast with the supply-led or product-orientated approach to planning, by which an organization develops products and then either simply supplies them (regulating the supply to an existing market) or creates a demand for them in the marketplace. In the context of library service, this can be equated with the library that makes decisions on stock selection or service provision without particular regard for customer need – unfortunately, a fairly common phenomenon.

The application of marketing principles to librarianship is covered, usefully, in *Modern library practice* edited by Sheila Ritchie.[27] Ritchie adapts to library service the classic tenets of marketing theory. She applies to library service planning the four basic stages of marketing:

- Define the market, i.e. determine the boundaries of the potential customer community. In the case of an academic library or an information unit in a commercial corporation this is probably a 'closed' community of all those who are connected directly with the organization. A public library has a more 'open' community of those who live, work or study within a particular local authority's geographic area.
- Analyse and segment the market, i.e. divide the customer community into identifiable groups. This process of market segmentation is common in commerce where groups are defined by gender, age, occupation, locality, type of housing, socioeconomic status, and so on. The principle can be applied to libraries: for example, in an academic library's segmentation of the customer community into academic staff and students, undergraduates and postgraduates, full-time and part-time, etc.; or in a public library's segmentation by age (preschool

49

children, youngsters, teenagers, adults, elderly people), by mobility (with special services to the housebound and institutionalized), by ethnicity (with services targetted to specific minority ethnic groups), or by various categories of 'disadvantage' (for example, unemployed people or adults with a need to develop basic literacy skills).

- Consider the market position, i.e. the library's position in relation to other agencies (in commercial parlance, the 'competition') working in the same marketplace. Are other agencies serving some of the library-related needs of any of the identified market segments? For example, in the area of community information, there may well be local agencies offering information and advice (Citizens Advice Bureau, Law Centre, Community Centre, etc., etc.). Should the library attempt to serve all of the identified market segments or should it assign priorities and identify key target sectors? What sectors is the library serving well – and what sectors does it wish to serve better?

- Assign priorities, coordinate the target market segments; plan services.

At this fourth stage, Ritchie applies the classic product-market matrix to library service development, identifying four strategies:

- Market penetration; increasing the use of existing services by existing customer groups.
- Market development; targetting new customer groups for existing services.
- Service development; offering new services to existing customer groups.
- Diversification; targetting new customer groups and offering new services.

Inherent in this process of planning services is the concept of the 'product life cycle' – the idea that new products grow, mature, peak, and then decline. The idea of discontinuing those services which are in decline is one which librarians find hard to deal with, perhaps because of the traditional custodial role of libraries. But the concept of discarding failures is central to the experimental approach to service planning and delivery. With widening possibilities for service, and constrained resources, those aspects of the service which are no longer supported by adequate custom must either adapt, or die.

Having moved from market research, through an assessment of priorities, to the identification and analysis of products, a marketing manager would then make decisions regarding the pricing, placing, and promotion of those products. This is also a useful checklist of considerations to be applied to library service.

Pricing can, of course, include the decision that a service should be supplied free of direct charge. However, all library services involve an element of 'pricing' – either a subscription or fee for the service itself (interlending requests, online searches, photo-copying, the borrowing of certain types of material, etc.), or fines charged for overdue items. Pricing is an important dimension of the current debate in the UK, stimulated by the government's consultative paper, *Financing our public library service: four subjects for debate*, over services for which a charge might be made and over the level of charges that might be made; should certain services be priced at marginal cost, at full economic cost, or at a level determined by 'market forces' which generates additional income? 'Value added' services and the possibilities for charging are also being debated by librarians in the USA.[28]

Placing can mean decisions about which libraries are to offer a particular new service; and it can also be interpreted to mean the whole issue of accessibility. Where is the service to be offered – in the library building or by 'outreach' through some other agency? When is the service to be offered? Are traditional 'office hours' sufficient, or should the service be available during evenings and at weekends? It would make sense in terms of customer access, for example, if public libraries in residential areas and academic libraries on residential campuses (or serving part-time students) were to open on Sundays.

Promotion includes the whole range of advertising, publicity and public relations (PR) techniques and strategies. Traditionally, libraries in the UK have not made good use of these, perhaps because of a rather passive, supply-led approach to service. But people use libraries voluntarily. Libraries, therefore, need strategies to gain attention, arouse interest and generate custom.

They need to promote the services offered, both directly to the customer and indirectly (in the case of public libraries) by developing good relations with the local media. They need to project a positive and attractive image – and meet the expectations thus raised with a high quality of service delivery. The importance of PR and promotion has, perhaps, been recognized more in the USA than the UK with American libraries and professional bodies developing a number of initiatives in this area. One is the influential 'Friends of the library' concept. As Sandy Dolnick writes[29] 'an organized Friends group is living proof of the library's value to its community'. Other initiatives relate to particular areas of service. Baskin and Harris, for example, writing on the 'mainstreaming' movement, emphasize the importance of 'aggressively' seeking out people with special needs to promote and explain the ways in which the library can serve them.[30]

The final element in the marketing approach is, of course, monitoring and evaluation. Whatever strategies have been followed – of market penetration, market development, service development, or diversification – their progress, and success, will need to be evaluated.

There is considerable current interest, in both the USA and the UK, in service quality as seen from the viewpoint of the customer. In Britain, the National Consumer Council has produced a series of reports on local authority services (including public libraries) under the general title of *Measuring up*.[31] These stress service *for* the consumer rather than *to* the consumer, and attempt to provide a framework with which to analyse the effectiveness of service from the consumer perspective. The Local Government Training Board has also focussed on this issue with a booklet and a range of training courses on *Getting closer to the public*.[32] The LGTB looks at service from the public's point of view, provides a framework for reviewing current practice, and suggests some strategies to make services more responsive to customers and local citizens. *Measuring up* offers support to consumers in assessing the quality of service. *Getting closer to the public* provides a useful set of frameworks for service providers. The result – as Figure 6 (taken from *Getting closer to the public*) indicates – is to bring a 'customer focus' to the whole management cycle.

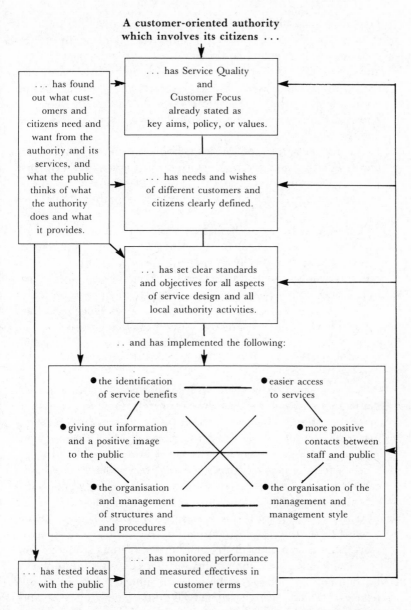

**A customer-oriented authority
which involves its citizens . . .**

... has found out what customers and citizens need and want from the authority and its services, and what the public thinks of what the authority does and what it provides.

... has Service Quality and Customer Focus already stated as key aims, policy, or values.

... has needs and wishes of different customers and citizens clearly defined.

... has set clear standards and objectives for all aspects of service design and all local authority activities.

.. and has implemented the following:

- the identification of service benefits
- giving out information and a positive image to the public
- the organisation and management of structures and and procedures
- easier access to services
- more positive contacts between staff and public
- the organisation of the management and management style

... has tested ideas with the public

... has monitored performance and measured effectivess in customer terms

**Figure 6: Management activities given a customer-orientated focus.
From *Getting closer to the public*, Local Government Training
Board, 1987, p.27.**

Defining customer requirements

A key element in the marketing approach is the definition of customer requirements and preferences – the demands, wants and needs of particular sectors of the customer community. This raises two difficult issues. How can library managers assess and anticipate customer requirements? And how do library managers know that the services being provided are valued by the customer community?

The first issue turns on the distinction between demands, wants, and needs – and on the difficulty of distinguishing between a service which is responding to customer need (market-led) and one which is providing what the professionals think the clients might want (supply-led).

A *demand* is overt – the act of *demanding* implies expression. However, it may not be explicit. A demand that the public library 'do something for the increasing numbers of elderly people in our community' or that an academic library 'do more for part-time students' is not precise enough to provide a basis on which to plan service. But it does at least identify a customer sector and signal the desirability of targetting services to that group of people. It triggers awareness and so initiates the process of analysis and investigation by which the planning and decision-making cycle commences.

A *want* may be keenly felt – but is not necessarily expressed. And a *need* may not even be consciously felt. How can customer-orientated service be developed in these instances? To give a practical example: some years ago, in a suburb of Birmingham, England, the local branch librarian noticed that many of the people who visited the library during the day were elderly people who came in alone. The librarian knew that many elderly people live on their own, and wondered if – behind their *demand* (expressed by borrowing books) – lay a *need*. Were some of these people lonely? Did they want companionship and the chance of conversation with other people? Did they *need* that companionship – would it improve the quality of their lives – without that unconscious *need* having yet become formulated into a consciously felt *want*? The branch library had a little-used meeting room and, with help from various volunteer agencies, the room was opened one morning a week as a 'drop in' centre with cups of tea and coffee, and the chance of a chat. The 'drop in' centre was well-used and much appreciated and became, for a period, an important element in the social fabric of that local group of elderly people.

This example illustrates the three key points in defining customer need. The first is to take advantage of existing statistical data in order to build up a profile of the customer community. One of the factors which triggered this chain of thought in the mind of the branch librarian was the discovery, from census data, that a significant percentage of the local population was made up of elderly people (i.e. those in receipt of a state pension) living alone.

This process of 'community profiling' does not apply just to public libraries. An academic library may well discover, from data on student intake, that the balance of full-time and part-time students in the institution is changing with increasing numbers of students attending courses in the evening or on one particular day each week. This has obvious implications for policies regarding opening times, loan periods, and so on.

The second point is the importance of experimentation. In commerce, it is usual when developing a new product or targetting a new market to run a 'test market' or 'pilot trial' in order to see if the idea works or iron out any 'teething troubles'. The only way to find out if the concept of the 'drop in' centre would work was to try it and see. Experimentation to test conjecture regarding possible customer wants and needs is akin to the 'systematic gambling' which Charles Handy puts forward as a means of dealing with a situation of discontinuous change.

Careful community profiling allied to a policy of experiment-ation should ensure that services have value in relation to the real needs of the customer community, and not just in the minds of library staff. The third point – which reinforces this – is the need for feedback from the customer community itself. There is considerable difficulty in gaining useful feedback directly from the customer community. In a 'closed' community like an academic institution or business corporation it is possible to identify a customer 'sample' which represents the market which has been targeted. In the context of a public library with its 'open' community this is much more difficult.

Even if the sample is a true representation of the whole community, it is difficult to get objective and accurate responses.

However carefully a questionnaire or structured interview is phrased in order to be non-directive and neutral, the accuracy and objectivity of the response can be affected simply by the fact that the respondent has been asked for his or her opinion. Customer feedback will always be subjective; conditioned by perceptions and expectations. The final difficulty with such surveys of customer attitudes and opinions is that they are time-consuming in preparation, implementation and analysis.[33]

However, such feedback, although not necessarily scientific, does provide valuable pointers. For example, a small-scale street survey, carried out in various districts of Birmingham during 1988, made it clear that many people – including many who described themselves as 'regular' library users (visiting a library once a month or more) – were not aware of the range of community information services offered by Birmingham's public libraries. It became clear that these services needed to be much more actively promoted both inside the libraries and to the community at large.

What is significant about this example is that it was a relatively 'quick and dirty' survey – a short verbal questionnaire administered to a random sample of willing passers-by on one particular day in six separate 'high street' locations within the Birmingham city boundary (generating around 300 responses). It was devised, under guidance, and administered and analysed by postgraduates studying for their professional qualification in librarianship; the time of library staff was taken up only with finalizing the form that the questionnaire would take and evaluating the students' conclusions. Yet the survey produced useful results – clear pointers to indicate areas of action and further investigation. Research, in order to be effective, does not necessarily have to be extensive or expensive. A regular process of feedback from customers – an inherent part, for example, of the planning and monitoring process developed by the ALA's Public Library Development Program – does not have to cost a great deal in terms of money or staff resources. Chapter 6, in discussing quality and value of library service, returns to the subject of user feedback.

Analysis of available data, a policy of systematic experiment-ation, and mechanisms for 'quick and dirty' indicative feedback from customers – all help in the continuous process of defining the requirements of the customer community.

Image and expectations

Customer feedback is subjective – shaped by perceptions and expectations regarding library service. Those perceptions and expectations condition customer attitudes and behaviour and are, in great measure, a product of the library's 'image'.

'Image' is at once superficial and fundamental. It is superficial because it does not always reflect reality: just as 'you can't judge a book by looking at the cover', so you can't gauge a library's effectiveness by its external appearance or by the fact that the staff are in business suits – or casually dressed. However, first impressions do count. Initial perceptions do precondition expectations, and may indeed influence the basic customer decision about whether to go in and use the library, or not.

Image is thus important in relation to customers. It is also important as a reflection and reinforcement of organizational culture; and for the impact which it can have on staff morale. It is therefore, very properly, a management concern. Considerations of the way in which the service is presented should be built into the planning process. Libraries and librarians have a poor public image, judged by the popular stereotype presented in fiction, films, cartoons, advertisements and so on. The content of that stereotype is clear:

● Staff. Demure girls, meek spinsters, elderly and crotchety women, wimpish or rather fey men.
● Location. Identified by hardback books on shelves, signs indicating 'Silence', and the librarian behind a large library counter wielding a date-stamp.
● Message. Libraries are dull and dusty, librarians are weak and unexciting people, library service is book-based, building-based, and bound by strict rules (silence, fines, etc.).

When the heroine of an early Beach Boys song cruises to the hamburger stand in her daddy's car, she forgets that she told her father she was going to the library.[34] On the one hand – fast cars, fast food, and 'fun, fun, fun'. On the other – the staid and boring world of parental control, and libraries.

Superman is a somewhat bumbling journalist, Indiana Jones

an academic and archaeologist; but to give a superhero or derring-do adventurer an alter ego as a librarian would be *too* improbable! It is discomfiting to suggest that much of this popular stereotype is justified. But anecdotal evidence, 'quick and dirty' investigation, and structured research all suggest that the image has some basis in reality.

Librarianship students at Birmingham Polytechnic, when they first arrive in the city, are asked to conduct an 'image audit' of local libraries. The aim is to analyse how the library 'feels' to a first-time customer; to assess how accessible (in physical, psychological and bureaucratic terms) the library is. Students are provided with a checklist of points to consider

- Siting: where is it? how do you find out? how do you get there?
- External appearance: how does it 'feel' from the outside? is it open? is it accessible?
- What happens when you get inside: what image does it present as you walk in? is it clear what to do and where to go? is there someone to ask? do they look welcoming?
- Using the library: is it easy to join? is it easy to use? do you get any help?
- Services: what services are provided? how do you find out?
- Layout: is the layout clear? are there adequate signs and guiding? are there different 'spaces' to do different things? how do the spaces 'feel'?

The results – like the 'quick and dirty' research mentioned earlier – cannot be said to be scientific; and it is clear that different people perceive the same things in different ways. One library, described as 'confused and messy' by one student, was seen as 'attractive and approachable' by another – both were commenting on its informality and bustle. But a useful set of points for consideration did emerge.

- Need for on-street signs. Libraries are not always easy to find.
- External appearance sometimes 'shabby' and/or 'intimidating'.
- Difficult physical access at some libraries – steps, heavy doors, etc.

- Interior environment sometimes poor – cold, badly lit, dingy decor, 'tatty' furnishings.
- Layout confusing; misleading (or non-existent) guiding; scruffy notices.
- Not always clear where to go to enquire about joining the library.
- Staff tendency to emphasize the rules (limits on number of books that can be borrowed, loan period, etc.) rather than explaining the services.

Comments about library staff ranged widely. Some staff were described as easily approachable, friendly and helpful. Others produced a negative reaction:

- 'Staff staring into space, arms folded.'
- 'Staff talking amongst themselves, ignoring users.'
- 'Sour-faced girl on the registration desk.'
- 'Girl behind the desk looked bored, fed up, and wanting to go home.'
- 'Staff seemed too busy to deal with enquirers' (this mentioned by several students).

Two points emerge from this. One is the importance of staff attitudes and appearance in determining customer perceptions and the 'quality' of the customer experience in the library. This is reinforced by Margaret Slater's research into the use of libraries in industry and commerce.[35] Slater's survey of industrialists showed that, while some respondents described the major characteristics of library staff in a positive way, there were many more negative comments about staff who seemed passive, apathetic, aloof, casual, incompetent, unworldly, over-conscientious, impatient, uncommunicative, ill-informed, etc. The popular stereotype of the librarian usually has public libraries in mind and the Birmingham student survey dealt mainly with public branch libraries (although a few academic libraries were also included). Slater's research suggests that the stereotype remains valid in specialized libraries. The issues raised by Slater's research will be discussed in Chapter 4.

The other point is the number of relatively minor details (scruffy signs, heavy doors, bad lighting, etc.) which are sometimes overlooked by library staff but which can cumulate into a powerful negative image. These points concerning staff attitudes and library details are of particular importance in providing library service for customers with special needs because of physical or mental disability. 'Mainstreaming' – bringing disabled people into the 'mainstream' of society – requires library managers to pay attention to all barriers (physical and psychological) which might inhibit use.[36]

There are a number of strategies which can help improve the library's image. The first is for management to recognize the need to give serious consideration – and an element of resourcing – to the way in which the service is presented. An 'image audit', such as that outlined above, provides a starting point.

A second concerns the library staff. Because 'people who feel good about themselves produce good results' and because staff attitudes form a significant part of the image presented, issues of staff deployment, development and motivation become relevant here. These will be discussed in Chapter 4.

A third concerns the 'culture' of the library service. Libraries exist to serve customers – and yet the Birmingham student survey and Slater's research both identified library staff who were perceived as being 'too busy' to deal with customers. In a truly market-led, customer-orientated service this would not happen. Staff would know – because of the culture and values transmitted throughout the organization – that direct service to the customer was their primary responsibility. This would be constantly reinforced in training sessions, appraisal interviews, on-job coaching, casual conversation, the example of senior staff, discussion at staff meetings, and so on. Issues to do with organizational 'culture' will be dealt with in the next chapter.

The fourth strategy involves building public relations (PR) into the planning process as a regular item for consideration. This encompasses issues such as:

● Considerations of the library's 'corporate identity', as trans-mitted through logos, letter-heads, signs, displays and other elements to which 'design' criteria could be applied.
● Advertising; does the library promote its events and services with posters and – even – paid-for advertising using the local media? Slogans and posters such as those developed

by the American Library Association ('Jog your mind – run to the library' ... 'Library – a word to the wise' ... 'The library is full of success stories' ... and so on) can be used at local level; and also provide cheery decor!

- Relations with the media; are these cordial and fruitful? is the 'media potential' of events always considered? are the media informed about what is going on? This applies to in-house media (staff magazines, etc.) as well as local newspapers, radio, etc. and so is a consideration for libraries in 'closed' communities as much as for public libraries. Does the library service get as much editorial coverage as it might?
- Public speaking (again, in-house as well as to external bodies); are opportunities sought to promote the service through talks and presentations? are staff trained and supported (e.g. by the production of graphics and audiovisual aids) in this area?
- Other opportunities to raise awareness and attract interest – by publications and other products; or by 'freebies' (balloons, badges, bookmarks, bags) and general razzamatazz. Sutton library hires out umbrellas for a nominal charge of 25 pence; on a rainy day up to 500 umbrellas with slogans promoting Sutton's library services are unfurled on the streets of this London suburb.

The aim of public relations is to further mutual understanding and cooperation between an organization and its various publics. Customer perceptions, staff morale, and resource allocation can all be affected by public opinion. Library managers need to plan a systematic strategy for positive PR incorporating the following stages:

- identifying the library's various publics;
- setting objectives for the PR programme;
- creating the communication;
- selecting the appropriate channel of communication;
- costing the programme;
- evaluating the programme.

The commercial world is well aware of the value of corporate PR. Managers are trained in skills relating to the media and public speaking. Organizational support is given in the shape of graphic artists, design consultants, and the promotion of a 'corporate identity'. Advertising is used, not just to sell products, but also to inform the public and generate external good will (and, in so doing, internal morale).

Like organizations in the commercial world, libraries are dependent on customers. In order to attract custom, libraries, like commercial organizations, need to raise awareness, build interest, develop understanding, and generate desire to use the service. Considerations of 'image' and strategies for corporate PR are central to that process.

References

1 See Sandy Dolnick (ed.), *Friends of libraries sourcebook*, Chicago, ALA, 1980.

2 The importance of the planning document is stressed in Charles R. McClure *et al.*, *Planning and role setting for public libraries: a manual of options and procedures*, Chicago, ALA, 1987, p.67.

3 *Ibid.*, p.57.

4 Kenneth Blanchard and Spenser Johnson, *The one minute manager*, Fontana/Collins, 1983, p.19.

5 Charles Handy, *Understanding organizations*, 3rd edition, Penguin, 1985, pp.410 – 11.

6 Thomas J. Peters and Robert H. Waterman, *In search of excellence*, New York, Harper and Row, 1982, p.319.

7 Niccolo Machiavelli, *The discourses*, ed. Bernard Crick, Penguin, 1970. Book Three, p.425f.

8 Leaflet summarizing *Advancing with knowledge: the British Library strategic plan, 1985 – 1990*, British Library, 1985.

9 OAL, *The future development of libraries and information services: progress through planning and partnership*, Library Information Series, number 14, HMSO, 1986.

10 See: Vernon E. Palmour *et al.*, *A planning process for public libraries*, Chicago, ALA, 1980.
Nancy A. Van House *et al.*, *Output measures for public libraries: a manual of standardised procedures*, 2nd edition, Chicago, ALA, 1987.
C. R. McClure *et al.*, *Planning and role setting for public libraries: a manual of options and procedures*, Chicago, ALA, 1987.

11 McClure *et al.*, *Planning and role setting*, p.28.

12 Palmour *et al.*, *A planning process . . .*, p.6.

13 Drucker, *The practice of management*, pp.356 – 7.

14 F. M. Cornford, *Microcosmographia academica: being a guide for the young academic politician*, Cambridge, Bowes and Bowes, 1908, 11th impression, 1983.

15 Roger Stoakley, *Presenting the library service*, Bingley, 1982, p.105.

16 Patricia Breivik, *Planning the library instruction program*, Chicago, ALA, 1982.

17 John Cowley, 'The development of library and information services in new academic institutions' in *The development of national library and information services*, ed. Edward Dudley, Library Association, 1983, p.184.

18 Andrew M. Pettigrew, *The politics of organizational decision-making*, Tavistock, 1973.

19 Terrell Blodgett, 'The city in 2000 AD: a microcosm of American democracy' in *Public library quarterly*, **7**, (Fall-Winter 1986), pp.9 – 25.

20 McClure, *Planning and role setting*, p.28.

21 John Blagden, *Do we really need libraries?*, Bingley, 1980, p.13.

22 Peggy Heeks and Paul Turner (eds.), *Public library aims and objectives*, PLRG, 1981.

23 Palmour *et al.*, *A planning process . . .*, p.57.

24 DES/OAL, 'Working together with a national framework', para. 8. Paper 2 of *The future development of libraries and information services*, Library Information Series no.12, HMSO, 1982.

25 C. R. McClure *et al.*, *Planning and role setting . . .*, Chicago, ALA, 1987.

26 A point stressed in Walter Goldsmith and David Clutterbuck, *The winning streak: Britain's top companies reveal their formulas for success*, Penguin, 1985.

27 Sheila Ritchie (ed.), *Modern library practice*, Elm Publications, Kings Ripton, 1982.

28 Linda Crismond, 'The future of public library service', in *Library journal*, **111**, (November 15, 1986), pp.42 – 9.

29 Sandy Dolnick (ed.), *Friends of libraries sourcebook*, p.2.

30 Barbara H. Baskin and Karen H. Harris (eds.), *The mainstreamed library: issues, ideas, innovations*, Chicago, ALA, 1982, p.188.

31 *Measuring up: paper 3, public libraries*, National Consumer Council, 1986.

32 *Getting closer to the public*, Local Government Training Board, Luton, 1987.

33 A useful discussion of customer surveys is provided by Sue Stone, *Library surveys*, revised 2nd edition, Bingley, 1982. They are also a key element of the planning process as described in Palmour *et al.*, *A planning process for public libraries*.

34 The Beach Boys, 'Fun, fun, fun' (Wilson-Love); from *Beach Boys Party*, Capitol/EMI, 1964.
35 Margaret Slater, *Non-use of library-information resources at the workplace*, Aslib, 1984.
36 A point stressed in Baskin and Harris (eds.), *The mainstreamed library*.

3 The dynamics of organization

Perspectives on organization

There are many ways of looking at organizations. When an individual starts a new job, for example, he or she needs to explore several different aspects of the organization's workings – its dynamics:

- What is the organizational hierarchy? How does the job fit in to the 'organization chart' – the diagram showing lines of command linking, through levels of responsibility and delegated authority, all the jobs in the organization.
- How are decisions made? What is the mechanism (for example, through a cycle of interlocking formal meetings)? What is the style – how much autonomy do individuals have on various levels of the hierarchy? How much consultation and participation in decision-making is there?
- How do communications 'flow' within the organization? Are they primarily written, or verbal? At a distance or face to face? 'Top down' or 'bottom up'?
- What informal networks are there? How does the 'grapevine' work? Who are the 'gate-keepers' who receive and pass on information informally? Are there equivalents of the 'King's Parade' – informal forums where information is exchanged and deals are done? How important – how powerful – is this 'hidden' organization?
- What is the style and 'feel' of the organization? What are the values it projects?

This checklist (by no means complete) illustrates a number of key points about organizations. There will be an explicit formal structure – but there will also be a 'hidden' informal complex of networks. There will be agreed mechanisms (for decision-making and communication), but there will also be a strong human dimension affecting the operation of these mechanisms. As well as issues of structure, the newcomer has to assimilate the 'culture' (style, 'feel', values) of the organization.

Organizations, then, are complex and dynamic entities. To analyse the various dimensions of this multifaceted concept, the study of organizations has drawn on a range of different perspectives. These can be presented in an historical and dialectic sequence of *thesis, antithesis* and *synthesis.*

Theories of organizational behaviour grew, initially, out of the Industrial Revolution and the development of the factory system.[1] The classic statement of this early approach was Frederick Taylor's *Principles of scientific management* (1911) which advocated the application of 'scientifically' deduced methods to the production process. Taylor's recognition that manufacturing processes can be systematically analysed and divided into a sequence of single tasks led to time-and-motion studies and the 'assembly line' concept. 'Scientific' management viewed the organization from an engineering perspective generally described as 'mechanistic' – the organization as machine. This provides the initial *thesis* of organizational theory.

However, this approach takes little account of the human dimension. People were seen as cogs in the machine, motivated by material rewards, and told what to do by management. An emphasis on 'human relations', emerging from the perspectives of social and behavioural sciences, provides the *antithesis* of this view.

The classic starting-point for the 'human relations' school is the so-called 'Hawthorne effect'. A series of experiments were conducted in the Western Electric Company's factory at Hawthorne, near Chicago, between 1924 and 1932. These were intended – in the manner of scientific management – to explore the relationship between working conditions (levels of lighting, structure of the working day, etc.) and productivity. What was discovered, however, was that production increased, not because of changed working conditions, but because the workers felt important and appreciated as the subject of scientific study. The 'Hawthorne effect' is the effect of making people feel special. It underpins the maxim already quoted that 'People who feel good

66

about themselves produce good results'.

This approach stresses the importance of individual psychology and social interaction. Motivation, the importance of peer-group relationships, the informal, 'hidden' networks of the organization – the dynamics of the organizations are analysed in terms of interpersonal relations.

Two examples have already been used, showing the insights that can result from the application of social/behavioural sciences to management studies. One is Mintzberg's research into the nature of a manager's work (Chapter 1). The other is Pettigrew's research into the political dimension of organizational decision-making (Chapter 2).

A number of studies offer a contrast – an implicit comparison of *thesis* and *antithesis* – between a 'scientific management' approach and a 'human relations' approach. Best known of these studies are three published in the early 1960s:

- McGregor's Theories X and Y.
- Likert's four-stage model of management styles.
- Blake and Mouton's management grid.

Douglas McGregor[2] contrasts two theories (which he terms 'X' and 'Y') about people in organizations. Theory X suggests:

- most people dislike work and will avoid it if possible.
- most people must, therefore, be pressured externally (persuaded, rewarded, punished, controlled) in order to get them to contribute towards organizational objectives.
- most people prefer to be led and directed, wish to avoid responsibility, have relatively little ambition, and are motivated by a need for security.

Theory Y suggests:

- people have within them the capacity for self-motivation and the potential to seek out and take on responsibility.
- people work best in a supportive environment which integrates personal goals and organizational objectives.

A manager who has 'theory X' assumptions about the workforce is likely to take a 'scientific management' task-centred, directive approach. A manager inclined to the 'theory Y' viewpoint is likely to operate in a more people-orientated, participative, 'human relations' manner.

Rensis Likert[3] distinguished four types of management style. The first two are authoritarian, one autocratic and exploitative, the second more benevolent. With these styles, the organizational structure is tall and narrow with centralized decision-making and little delegation. Likert's third style is consultative. Staff are asked their opinions which may, or may not, be taken into account when decisions are made. The fourth style is genuinely participative with the work group sharing their views and making decisions collectively.

The 'managerial grid' developed by Robert Blake and Jane Mouton[4] provides a framework within which to compare the relative value given by a manager to 'concern for people' and 'concern for production'. At the end of the latter scale is an over-riding concern for output and efficiency. At the end of the former scale is a 'country club' approach with comfortable personal relations, a relaxed pace of work, and low concern for output. The '1.9' position (the 'country club' approach) is excessively orientated towards human relations. The '9.1' position (concern for output above all) is excessively mechanistic. A midpoint on the grid shows a 'middle of the road' approach ensuring adequate output and satisfactory morale. A high score on both scales (the so-called '9.9' position) indicates an excellent performance in terms of both interpersonal relations and work output.

Useful reviews of these theories, applying them to library work, are contained in *Staff management in library and information work* by Noragh Jones and Peter Jordan and in *Library management* by Robert Stueart and John Taylor Eastlick.[5]

Management style is often described in terms of a continuum of possibilities from *autocratic* to *democratic* – from authoritarian to participative. In reviewing work done in this area, Charles Handy[6] uses the more useful distinction between *structuring* and *supportive* styles. This less emotive terminology gives a positive value to both types of approach. Structure, direction, clear mechanisms and a focus on the job to be done are needed; so too is support for the individual, an awareness of social processes,

68

and recognition of the 'psychological contract' between individual and organization.

There is, then, a need for *synthesis* between the 'mechanistic' perspective and the 'social/behavioural' perspective. This is currently provided by the 'systems' approach to organizations. The perspective here is partly biological or ecological – the organization seen as an organism, evolving and adapting as a result of internal and external stimuli – and partly that of systems theory as developed in computing and cybernetics.

The organization is seen as a system consisting of two principal subsystems. The 'technical' subsystem incorporates the 'mechanistic' elements: plant and machinery, work-flow, routines and processes, etc. The 'social' subsystem includes the 'human relations' dimension. Both co-exist and management must give due regard to both.

The standard representation of an organization as system (see Figure 7) includes inputs, processes, outputs and a 'control' loop providing feedback on outputs in order to regulate and adapt inputs and processes. However, organizations do not have built-in mechanisms of feedback and control, as do certain machines. Nor do they have automatic processes of adaptation and evolution, as do animals and other organisms.

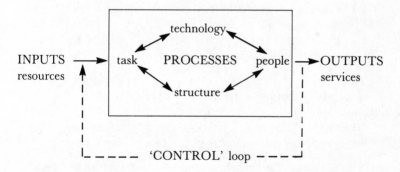

Figure 7: The organization as system

Organizations need to introduce sophisticated communications systems in order to simulate this feedback/control/adaptation process. A central point in Peter Drucker's *Innovation and entre-*

69

preneurship is the importance of information flow into and within the organization. Drucker notes[7] that the model of technology has shifted from mechanical processes to biological processes organized around information. There is currently considerable interest in the nature of organizations as information systems, from the perspective of computing and cybernetics (that is, the science of systems of control and communications; in particular, study of the human control system of nervous system and brain, and experimentation with applications of computing technology to intelligent processes).

The systems approach implies two important points. The first is that an organization is a dynamic, changing entity. It is never static. An organization chart may appear to show a fixed structure, but a fixed framework still allows for considerable freedom and flexibility of organizational behaviour – and the structure itself will adapt over time. The second is that there is no one 'best' form of organization. Rosemary Stewart[8] sees the major contribution of social sciences to the understanding of organizations as being this awareness: 'that different types of behaviour need different forms of organization and that the appropriate kinds of organization can change with the company's situation.'

This 'contingency' theory – that is, the theory that the nature of an organization is contingent upon its situation – reinforces the importance of information. Tom Lupton (who has made a particular study of the impact of social science theories on management) points out:[9]

Any theory about design which rests on the principle 'it all depends' is bound to be more complex than one which rests on supposedly universally applicable injunctions. To accept a 'contingent' theory as a practical guide is to face the challenge of identifying and measuring the contingent factors.

The 'systems' approach and the concept of the 'adaptive' organization (that is, the organization as open system or organism, adapting to meet changing circumstances) is very relevant to libraries. As organizations, libraries clearly illustrate the co-existence of technical and social subsystems. In terms of service delivery these concepts are formalized in the traditional structural division, in academic libraries, between 'technical services'

70

(relatively mechanical – and nowadays often automated – processes of acquisition, cataloguing, circulation control and so on) and 'reader services' (services involving the social process of interaction between staff and customers).

The library needs to be 'adaptive' given a context of discontinuous change. The customer community, the library's governing framework, and a range of external considerations all form 'contingent factors' to be taken into account.

Finally, libraries, like other adaptive organizations, need good information systems. These are necessary partly because of the point mentioned by Lupton – in order to adapt to contingencies, an organization needs a continuous flow of information about the contingent factors surrounding it. They are also necessary as feedback/control mechanisms. The pressure of accountability requires that management demonstrate efficient use of resources, effective service delivery, and value to the customer. Management information systems are needed in order to achieve this aim, and these will be discussed in Chapter 6.

Issues of structure

Changes in size, new patterns of service provision, and the impact of information technology have all produced a considerable amount of restructuring of library organizations in recent years. Many public library departments in the UK have been restructured into larger directorates – of leisure, recreation, education, culture, etc. An emerging pattern in some British and American higher education institutions is the linking of library services with computer services to provide one integrated support network of information systems and services.[10] In schools and colleges, libraries have, in many instances, become part of a wider structure of 'learning resources'.

These changes in size reflect changes in the pattern of service provision; each is designed to provide a clearer direction and focus. So, in theory, the fundamental purpose of a UK public library within a 'leisure' ethos is distinct from that of a public library in 'education' – although, in practice, sharp distinctions in public library service, arising from their directorate contexts, are not yet evident. In educational establishments, however, there is a clearer link between this organizational restructuring and the nature and purpose of library service. The concept of the library

71

as a 'learning resource', for example, gives structural reinforcement to the view that a school or college library is the 'foundation of the curriculum' – a central part of the educational process, providing resources to enable students to develop learning skills.[11]

In public libraries, the link between structural change and the pattern of service provision is more at 'grass roots' level than directorate level, with the development of the 'community librarian' approach. Sheila Ritchie links the community-orientated approach to service with a consequent need to restructure the library organization.[12] Ritchie contrasts a passive, building-based approach to service with a more pro-active, developmental approach which gets much closer to the customer community and seeks to meet *need* as well as expressed *demand*. The latter, she suggests, requires a decentralized structure with participative decision-making, 'bottom up' communication, and delegated authority. Her implication is that the passive, building-based approach is delivered through a centralized structure with management mechanisms which are essentially 'top down'.

An important point here is the distinction between geographic decentralization and managerial decentralization. Public library structures have always been decentralized to a degree, provided through a geographic scatter of branch libraries. However, the management structure has often remained highly centralized with branch librarians having very little real delegated authority. Indeed, the term '*branch* library' is a literal statement of the management structure – the library as the local branch of a centrally-determined service.

In England, some local authorities – particularly some London boroughs – are developing a decentralized approach to services which are not, traditionally, delivered directly at local level: social services, for example, or housing repairs. Islington, for instance, is evolving a pattern of 'Neighbourhood Offices', each serving a local population of between 4,500 to 8,000 people. By bringing services to this 'neighbourhood' level, the local authority hopes to avoid the problems which are often attributed to centralized services – inefficiency, remoteness, inaccessibility, lack of responsiveness. In order to do this, the 'neighbourhood' concept does not just decentralize service delivery; it also decentralizes management authority. Each Neighbourhood Office, and service

72

department within that Office, has a considerable degree of autonomous authority for decision-making and resource allocation. Indeed some local authorities, including Islington, are developing mechanisms for involving local residents, directly, in decision-making at neighbourhood level.[13]

As well as changes in size and in patterns of service delivery, changes in technology are also having an impact on the structure of library organizations. In order to take full advantage of technological opportunities there is a need to build 'systems' skills into the management team. The automation of 'housekeeping' processes and technical services can mean a reduction in the number of staff employed in these areas. The possibilities for the development of new, IT-based, services can mean the emergence of new elements in the organization chart – staff responsible for online searching, database creation (for example, the provision of community information using videotex), or the 'repackaging' of information into state-of-the-art reports, current awareness bulletins and SDI services.

Technology may affect the process of communication between staff as well as the staffing structure. Networking and electronic mail offer opportunities for improved interactive communications across a geographically scattered organization and this may have an impact on participation in the decision-making process. These issues will be addressed more fully in Chapter 5.

Technology raises a further issue which has an impact on the structure of library organizations; the balance between what is provided from within the organization and what is contracted out to external agencies. Much of the 'behind the scenes' work of processing and cataloguing, for example, is no longer carried out within libraries. It is handled externally by bibliographic cooperatives (cataloguing) and commercial suppliers of library stock (processing). Indeed, some commercial suppliers are now offering a full range of bibliographic services including facilities for stock editing and collection development. There is thus no longer any need for a large section of the organizational structure to be devoted to bibliographic services and stock processing.

Similarly, electronic publishing and document delivery is changing the structure of reference/information services. Online information, interlending networks and facsimile transmission are – to a varying degree in different types of library – replacing or supplementing library holdings of printed books and other documents. Again, the balance changes between what is directly provided (in printed form) and services which enable the library to gain access (electronically) to information held elsewhere. Structural change in the balance between 'providing' and 'enabling' is becoming a highly significant issue for public libraries in the UK as the government extends the application of compulsory tender testing to local authority services.

This discussion of current structural issues illustrates three key points. The first is that a 'structure' cannot be regarded as a fixed and unchanging framework. Changes in size, service provision, technology, the balance between 'providing' and 'enabling' – all are 'contingent factors' which impact on and influence the library's evolving structure.

The second is that an organization's 'structure' serves a number of purposes. The organization chart indicates the reporting structure – the lines of command (of authority and accountability) necessary in order to coordinate and control the work of the organization. Another diagram might be needed to indicate lines of communication – for example, the horizontal lines of communication between staff on the same management level but in different parts of the organization which will not be shown in hierarchical lines of command.

As well as coordination/control and communication, the structure needs to incorporate a 'development' dimension, if service delivery is to be pro-active and customer orientated. A further diagram might be needed to indicate the ways in which people come together in order to plan service and think ahead.

The third point is that these purposes are sometimes, seemingly, in conflict. Consider the following checklists:

coordination	division
control	delegation
accountability	autonomy
stability	innovation
conformity	creativity

These are all desirable characteristics. The work needs to be divided up in an appropriate manner – yet it also needs to be coordinated and integrated to a common purpose. In order to get 'close to the customer' there is a need to delegate authority so that staff dealing directly with customers have some autonomy – yet there is a need to provide mechanisms for overall control and accountability to senior management. A pro-active and 'adaptive' organization will wish to support innovation and creativity – yet there has also to be a measure of stability and conformity to accepted procedures, agreed objectives and shared values. Essentially, this is a conflict between elements of centralization and decentralization. A major challenge for those library managers involved in any restructuring exercise is to keep these elements in balance.

The lines of command and the characteristics expressed in the left-hand checklist (above) operate through hierarchy and bureaucracy. The hierarchy enables everyone in the organization to know to whom they are accountable and for whom they are responsible. The bureaucracy lays down rules and procedures.

The hierarchy expresses the levels of power and authority from Chief Executive to the bottom rung on the corporate 'ladder'. The following illustrates how this reporting structure might look for a library assistant in a public and an academic library:

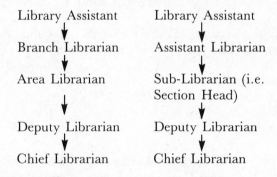

In both (rather simplified) cases, the hierarchy has five levels: the Chief and Deputy as senior management; the Area Librarian or 'Sub-Librarian' (a curious term used in UK universities) as middle management; and the Branch Librarian or Assistant Librarian as junior, line management.

One of the challenges of organizational structure is to keep the line of command as short and tight as possible by reducing to a minimum the number of levels in the hierarchy. This is a

75

challenge because of the need to keep each individual manager's 'span of control' – the number of people for whom that manager is responsible – within manageable proportions. In the example above it might be possible to remove from the public library hierarchy the middle-management level of Area Librarian, but all the Branch Librarians would then report directly to senior management. This is fine in a relatively small public library organization. But if the organization is large – say, of four areas each containing six branches – then the Deputy and Chief would have 24 Branch Librarians reporting directly to them. In terms of the span of control it would probably be more effective to retain the Area Librarians.

There is, then, a need to consider three points when examining the hierarchy of an organization

- overall size of the organization
- levels in the hierarchy
- spans of control for individual managers.

A fourth point which has a crucial impact on organizational structure – and which relates to the right-hand checklist (division, delegation, etc.) – is the need to divide the work to be done into a number of departments. Traditionally, there are four ways[14] in which this can be done

- by function
- by product
- by territory
- by customer group.

The classic division of public library work is by function – reference, lending, bibliographic services, etc. – and by territory, through a structure of branch libraries. In academic libraries there will be an element of functional division (bibliographic services, interlibrary loan, circulation desk, etc.) and also some division by customer group with the establishment of subject-based departments within the library. Public libraries also divide work on the basis of customer groups; traditionally with the division between adult and children's services and, more recently, with the targetting of services to particular customer groups – elderly

76

people, unemployed people, people from particular minority ethnic groups, etc. Finally, there is also some division by product – for example, music libraries, community information services, current awareness bulletins, etc. The fact that libraries use all four ways of dividing work into departments illustrates the complexity of library organizations and the difficulty of finding a structure which integrates all elements to meet service objectives.

Departmental separatism – by which the organization fragments into several departments which rarely communicate with each other – can be a characteristic of large library systems. There is no real communication between 'central' and 'the branches', between sites or subject libraries, between technical and reader services, etc. Equally, it can be experienced by the library itself in its relations with the other parts of the parent organization. In some large corporations, the library can appear bypassed and marginalized as the web of corporate communications and decision-making processes seems not to include the library staff.

There are a number of ways by which departmental separatism can be avoided. One is through a formal system of meetings and committees where staff from different departments come together. Similarly, interdepartmental project teams and 'task forces' can be set up to tackle particular initiatives and programmes. A third, less formal, strategy is that of individual managers 'networking' across the organization; building up personal contacts in a number of departments.

A further way of providing integration – and also an important element of professional development for the individual job-holder – is by creating a 'matrix' structure. This gives individuals a 'line' management function – for example responsibility for a particular service point – and also membership of a 'team'; for example, the team of librarians charged with providing service within a particular geographic area. The job description will give an indication of the relative proportion of time to be spent in each role (say, 60% line management, 40% team membership). A more sophisticated matrix may link the individual librarian to a particular territory (area team), a specific service (for example, children's services or reference work), and a section of stock (such as adult fiction). In this structure, the day-to-day administration of service points is likely to be delegated to Senior Library

Assistants, thus creating an element of career progression for non-professional staff. One value of 'team librarianship' as developed in public libraries is that it can help to break down barriers of departmental separatism; as well as offering a cost-efficient means of deploying professional staff.

A number of other 'teams' will exist within the organization contribute to the process of integration/coordination and to the process of planning and forward development. There will be a Management Team of senior staff. There will also be various 'expert' teams bringing together staff with a particular area of expertise; for example, a team responsible for developing staff training programmes or for a particular area of service delivery – children's services, online searching, etc. In addition to these permanent or long-term teams, there will be teams brought together for a relatively short time to plan a particular project or deal with a specific task; for example, the implementation of an automated circulation control system. As well as breaking down departmental separatism by bringing together staff from different sections in order to tackle a common objective, these teams also bring an element of flexibility and innovation into the organization's bureaucratic framework.

The concept of *bureaucracy* tends to get a bad press because of an association with complex regulations and procedures ('red tape') which tends to stifle initiative and promote inertia. But bureaucracy has positive values, in that it instills rationality and continuity into an organization. Bureaucracy is expressed through:

- specialization; structure shaped by job functions, not by particular individuals.
- stratification; hierarchy providing defined levels of authority.
- systems; of rules and procedures.

As well as an element of stability and consistency, the bureaucratic approach (a.k.a. 'correct channels' or 'the proper procedures' or 'playing it by the book') also leads to impersonality – and thus to fairness and equality of treatment. Bureaucracy can be a safeguard against arbitrary and over-personalized dealing and decision-making. However, bureaucracy can lead to an over-emphasis on rules, procedures and conformity.

There are two strategies which can help to inject a capacity for innovation and adaptation into the necessary bureaucratic framework. One is the use of short-term teams. The other is described by E. F. Schumacher as the fundamental task of achieving 'smallness' within an organization.[15]

'Smallness' is designed to avoid the problems normally associated with large organizations:

- remoteness and lack of commitment; an individual's feelings of personal responsibility for the success of the organization diminish as the organization grows.
- disaffection arising from the feeling of being 'just a cog in the machine'.
- 'red tape', inflexibility, delay, inertia (i.e. bureaucracy).

In terms of organizational structure, 'smallness' is achieved by decentralizing the organization into a number of small, relatively autonomous units. Library organizations are usually decentralized in structure – into a number of relatively small departments or branches – although management tends to remain centralized so that these small units have little real autonomy.

A particular value of 'smallness' and the use of teams is the sense of 'team spirit' that can be generated. Group dynamics and the generation of team spirit emphasize the importance of seeing an organization's structure as a *social* system as well as a *technical* system. Bureaucracy and the organization chart may be impersonal, but the success of an organization – the quality of library service – depends on people. As Tom Peters and Nancy Austin put it:[16]

> You can *order* the average person who reports to you to come to work five days a week and work his or her eight-and-a-half-hour day. But you *cannot* order *anyone* to perform in an *excellent* fashion – 'excellent' meaning courteous, creative. Excellence, by its very definition and at all levels, is a purely *voluntary* commitment.

There is a link between changing patterns of service provision and changing organizational structures. But structure alone does not determine the nature and quality of service. In order to bring in the 'people' dimension, considerations of structure need to be supplemented by the concept of organizational 'culture'.

The 'hidden' organization and the concept of 'culture'

The concept of organizational 'culture' is difficult to describe with precision because, unlike structure, it cannot be codified into a series of organization charts, a cycle of meetings, or a manual of procedures – although part of it can sometimes be captured in an organization's mission statement or set of core values. 'Culture' has already been mentioned a number of times in this book:

- the impact on management thinking of the 'enterprise culture' vigorously promoted in the UK by the present government.
- the development of an organizational 'culture' which puts the customer first.
- the need, in an adaptive organization, for a 'culture' which stimulates innovation, supports individual initiative, and accepts risk-taking; and which gives a 'bottom up' as well as a 'top down' dynamic to communications and decision-making.
- the 'loose-tight' concept of individual autonomy and self-control within the framework of a strong corporate 'culture' which constantly reinforces a few key values.
- the McKinsey 7-S Framework which puts 'shared values' at the centre of those things to which management should pay attention.

These examples suggest that culture is, at bottom, attitudinal. It is a set of attitudes – feelings, beliefs, values – which shape, and are reinforced by, actions. It is thus at the heart of the organization's social system.

In all organizations the formal structure co-exists with an informal, 'hidden' set of dynamics. One example has already been seen: the informal but influential 'politicking' based on the 'King's Parade', which co-exists with the formal decision-making structure. One aspect of the 'hidden' organization, then, is the informal power structure of *influence* which co-exists with the formal power structure of *authority*.

Traditionally, this 'hidden' organization has been developed and reinforced through the social relationships which evolve within peer groups; and through the history and heritage – the corporate memory – of an organization. It finds expression in the emergence of 'cliques' (tight knots of people who commune closely together, often to the exclusion of colleagues), the existence of an informal communications 'grapevine', and the establishment of 'unwritten rules'. These are an important guide to the workings and attitudes of the 'hidden' organization and cover issues such as

- who to approach for information or advice on a particular issue.
- how to communicate with colleagues; when to write, or phone, or go to see someone.
- how to address colleagues; first names, or a more formal approach.
- dress codes; shirt sleeves? ties (properly tied, or loosened?)? jeans? skirts or trousers? etc.
- at work early or late; a sign of diligence – or inefficiency?

These 'hidden' dynamics are a powerful force in socializing individuals into the 'norms' – the accepted attitudes and behaviour – of the organization.

This 'hidden' organization has considerable value. It provides peer group support, extends communication networks, and so can assist with the smooth operation of the organization. Rosemary Stewart suggests that it can even be responsible for the continued existence of organizations which would otherwise have collapsed; people develop informal methods of coping when organizations fail to adapt, formally, to changed circumstances.[17]

The 'hidden' organization, because it is based on social relationships, is naturally organic and adaptive. What is important, from the management perspective, is that these 'hidden' dynamics do not get out of line with the formal structure and objectives of the organization. A successful – and happy – organization is a single community where formal mechanisms and informal, 'hidden' dynamics work in harmony, mutually reinforcing each other. When this happens the organization can be said to have evolved a healthy and coherent 'culture'.

Charles Handy's *Understanding organizations*, which focusses on the 'psychology' of organizations and the people who work in them, offers a useful typology of organizational cultures.[18]

The *power* culture is entrepreneurial and competitive. There is little bureaucracy and much individual autonomy.

Communication is verbal, decision-making is a highly 'political' process based on the power of individual personalities. People are judged on results. This is a thrusting and dynamic culture which can work well in small organizations and at a time of rapid change. However, size can be a problem. Handy uses the image of a *web* to portray this culture – and the web can break if it gets too big or tries to link together too many activities.

The *role* culture suits large organizations operating in a stable environment. Power is based on position in the formal hierarchy. There is a clear structure of departmental responsibilities and bureaucratic procedures. It is important that individuals follow the correct process. This culture offers security and predictability, but change in the external environment can be a problem. Handy's image is of a *Greek temple* – and the foundations become insecure when the ground shakes.

Task culture is focussed on getting the job done. People and resources are brought together into project groups or task forces to 'get on with it'. Within the group power is based on expertise. Handy's image is of a *net* or *network*. This culture is good where flexibility, adaptability and responsiveness are needed. However it does not lend itself to control/coordination or to building strength in depth. It also needs an appropriately bountiful resource environment. When resources become limited, senior management has to control methods as well as results, and teams begin to compete, using political influence, for available resources. The *task* culture changes to a *role* or *power* culture.

This analysis of the resource environment's impact on organizational culture is particularly relevant to library service where, currently, there are often severe resource constraints. The *task* culture can provide the adaptability and innovation needed at a time of discontinuous change – hence the use of matrix structures and temporary teams within library organizations. But the need to allocate resources in a context of competing priorities shifts the emphasis to a *role* or *power* culture. Decisions have to be taken which will be unpopular with some people. A current difficulty within library management is to reconcile these conflicting cultures.

Considerations of organizational culture have to take into account the 'psychological contract' between the individual and the organization. This is the 'hidden' contract, based on

82

expectations and motivation, which co-exists with the formal contract of employment. As Handy explains:[19]

> This psychological contract is essentially a set of expectations. The individual has a set of results that he expects from his organization, results that will satisfy certain of his needs and in return for which he will expend some of his energies and talents. Similarly the organization has its set of expectations of the individual and its list of payments or outcomes that it will give to him.

This concept will be discussed further in the next chapter. But, clearly, an important element in this 'contract' is affinity between the culture of the organization and an individual's expectations and aspirations. An individual with a need for security will feel comfortable within a *role* culture. This might feel stifling to an individual with a need for recognition and 'self actualization' (that is, 'stretching' oneself to realize one's full potential); that person might have the strength, confidence and ruthlessness to operate successfully in a *power* culture. On the other hand, an individual with a need for group affiliation or the expression of expertise might find the most suitable niche in a *task* culture.

When managing change and dealing with the restructuring of organizations, it is important to remember the interaction between organizational culture and individual psychology. A change in culture can have a profound effect on the 'psychological contract' which conditions the attitudes and behaviours of individuals within the organization.

Handy's typology includes a fourth culture – the *person* culture in which the structure or organization only exists to serve the cluster of individuals within it. Handy suggests that barristers' chambers, architects' partnerships, hippy communes, small consultancy practices, families and similar organizations can have this *person* orientation. In this culture, influence is shared and when power is exercised it is on the basis of expertise. Handy makes the important point that, although there are few organizations where this culture predominates, there are many individuals whose personal preference is for this type of approach:[20] 'Specialists in organizations – computer people in business organizations, consultants in hospitals, architects in city government – often feel little allegiance to the organization but regard it rather as a place to do their thing with some accruing benefit to the main employer'.

This cast of mind is relevant to library service for two reasons. First, because of the increasing number of non-librarian specialists being employed within library organizations – people with expertise in systems, marketing, personnel, finance, administration, etc. – whose 'psychological contract' with the library may be shaped by this viewpoint. Second, because librarians themselves can think in this way. As specialists with a particular expertise their expectations and aspirations may well be framed in terms of 'the profession' rather than the organization in which they find themselves currently working. This is one possible reason for the barriers which can build up, in some libraries, between professional and non-professional staff. The latter think of their work in relation to the organization and, ideally, the customer community; and they sometimes perceive professional staff as being more interested in furthering their professional careers than in serving the needs of that library and its customers.

There are a number of factors which can determine the culture of an organization:

- the size of the organization;
- the age and history of the organization;
- the organization's purpose, objectives and activities;
- the resource environment within the organization;
- external environments which form 'contingent factors' for the organization;
- the people in the organization; their expectations, aspirations and motivation.

From this list it is clear that there can often be a mix of different cultures within the same organization. For example, the activities of a cataloguing department lend themselves to a culture – thoughtful and precise application of rules suggesting a *role* culture – different from that of a team of community librarians, where a strong focus on the team and the job suggests a *task* culture. The list also suggests that organizational cultures change over time and through changing circumstances. Cultural change, however, can be a slow and sometimes painful process, bound up as it is with the need for attitudes and behaviours to change.

To operate successfully within an organization, a manager needs to understand the dynamics of how that organization works. Those dynamics are based not just on the formal structure but also on the 'hidden' organization which co-exists with it. Structures are made up of people, and the manager needs to be aware of the psycho-dynamics of individuals, interpersonal relations, and groups. It is this psychological dimension which drives the attitudes and values underpinning the concept of organizational culture.

'Soft is hard'

This focus on culture and the 'hidden' organization of social relationships is a central concern of what might be termed the 'excellence' school of management writing – American books like *In search of excellence* by Peters and Waterman or *A passion for excellence* by Peters and Austin; or, in the UK, *The winning streak* by Goldsmith and Clutterbuck.[21] These books analyse successful companies to see if common characteristics emerge. Each emphasizes the importance of 'people' considerations if high quality results are to be achieved. To borrow a term used in the *Excellence* books, 'soft is hard' – the 'soft' human concerns determine the 'hard' outcomes, the performance of the organization.

Behind the hyperbole and vibrant language, there are a number of key points:

- The manager as coach, not just devising plans, but motivating people by careful and detailed attention to them as individuals.
- The manager as value-shaper, reiterating and reinforcing the core values of the organization by speech and action.
- The need for managers to 'walk the talk'; to show integrity and consistency – practise what they preach – in order to shape values and motivate individuals.
- The need for managers to get around the workplace, visibly and approachably. The *Excellence* books all stress the value of MBWA (Managing By Wandering Around). In addition this 'wandering around' – in the customer community as well as within the organization itself – keeps a manager in close touch with current situations and information to which the organization may have to respond or adapt.

- The importance of 'small stuff' – the succession of brief encounters that characterize the manager's day of, in Mintzberg's phrase, 'brevity, variety and fragmentation'.

Making the best use of these brief encounters is the fundamental message of *The one minute manager* by Blanchard and Johnson which stresses the importance of brief ('one minute') but effective sessions of goal-setting, praising, and reprimand.[22]

Books like the *Excellence* sequence and *The one minute manager* are sometimes dismissed as 'pop' management. In fact, they present – in clear and often vibrant language – fundamental insights into the dynamics of organizations and the psychology of individuals at work. The three issues on which *The one minute manager* focusses (goal-setting, praising, reprimand) are, for example, core elements in the process of 'developing people' which Peter Drucker sees as an essential part of a manager's job.

In search of excellence and *The winning streak* both offer a checklist of the key attributes of 'excellent' organizations. Although these attributes appear in different sequences, are expressed in different terminologies, and refer to different nations (the USA in one, the UK in the other), there is considerable consensus regarding the characteristics of successful organizations. What follows is a synthesis of those attributes, arranged under four main headings

- Purpose
  - clear sense of the fundamentals of the business
  - clear objectives
  - no dilution by diversification
- Market orientation
  - continuous market research
  - feedback from customers
  - care for quality control and customer service
  - integrity in dealing with customers
  - care to develop a good public image
- Organization
  - structure
    - kept simple
    - few staff at headquarters; most out 'in the field'
    - decentralized, with delegated authority and considerable autonomy

    – control
        – concern for the planning process
        – clear objectives, with feedback on results
        – constant reinforcement of core values
    – culture
        – 'hands on' involvement by managers: to transmit core values, and to generate commitment, enthusiasm and pride
        – attitudes supportive of innovation and entrepreneurship: a positive attitude to risk-taking (with tolerance of mistakes as part of the learning process); a bias for action and experimentation – try it out, get it done.

● People
    – productivity through people
        – respect for the individual
        – care for the motivation and morale of individuals
        – recognition that 'rank and file' staff are the root source of efficiency and quality of service
    – leadership
        – visible management (e.g. MBWA)
        – creation of an environment which encourages the exercise of leadership at all levels of management

This checklist provides a useful summary of the key issues raised in this book so far. It also illustrates how much organizational dynamics are intertwined with the psychology of people. Implicit throughout the checklist, for example, is the connection between excellent organizational performance and good interpersonal communications.

The importance of communications
The *Excellence* literature illustrates the link between communications and organizational performance. *The one minute manager* shows the link between communications and effective management. In these books, the focus tends to be on management communication which is ad hoc and verbal. Every organization will also contain two other types of communication: the formal communications structure, usually of meetings and memoranda; and the informal 'grapevine'. It is important for managers to realize that, however much an organization becomes

a single community, there will always be a network of communication and social relationships from which management is excluded.

Ken Jones suggests[23] that these informal communications networks play a vital role in easing the 'psycho-social strain' which individuals can experience in a bureaucratic organization. They do this in three ways:

- as a socializing force, giving people a sense of 'belonging', of being a member of the group with whom they communicate.
- as a part of the 'politicking' process, enabling people to attempt to influence the decision-making process.
- as an information network, transmitting news more rapidly than the 'official channels'.

The informal 'grapevine' is also, of course, one of the key ways in which an organization's culture is developed and reinforced. Stories circulate through the grapevine and then become part of the 'oral history' of the organization to be reiterated from time to time. These will inevitably focus on an individual or an event in a way which promotes certain values and attitudes.

Formal communications usually exist on paper. The written document provides a record and tends to be worded more precisely than a verbal interchange. Of course, simply writing and sending a message is no indication that the message has been received or understood or acted on. There is no (immediate) feedback. However, much communication in organizations tends to be of this one-way, paper-based type – memos, reports, bulletins of 'routine instructions' to all staff.

Meetings form the other major element of formal communication – regular committees, or specially convened meetings. There may well be considerable verbal interaction at these meetings, but the official record of discussions and decisions will be the 'minutes', a document written up afterwards and formally approved at the next meeting. Discussion will also have been largely limited to those items included on a preset 'agenda' of issues for consideration.

This formal, bureaucratic process is important – it provides a stable, impersonal and regular means by which issues can be raised and decisions made. But it is likely to be somewhat slow and ponderous. The vast majority of useful communications will take place *around* these meetings, rather than *in* them.

Communications within an organization can be described in terms of four directions:

- downward, following the hierarchical chain of command.
- upward, through a variety of mechanisms: reporting systems designed to monitor performance; participative planning and decision-making structures; the machinery of consultation and negotiation with trade union representatives.
- horizontally across, between peers in the same work groups, or departments and individuals on the same level of the hierarchy.
- diagonally across, for example when a department in one part of the organization needs the assistance of a senior specialist from another section.

In each direction there can be barriers to good communication. Within the hierarchy the quality of communication can diminish as it filters down – or up – through the chain of command. The desire to spread only good news gets in the way of full and accurate upward communication; information is 'laundered' as it passes higher up the hierarchy. A sense of status and of 'only telling people what they need to know' can obstruct the flow of information downward. This can lead to what has been described as the 'mushroom management' syndrome – people are kept in the dark and occasionally get a pile of fertiliser (or something similar) dumped on them.

In libraries, the split between professional and non-professional staff can lead to breakdowns in communication based on hierarchy. Non-professional staff are rarely included in the organization's cycle of formal meetings and are heavily dependent on their line manager – often a relatively recently qualified professional in a junior management position – in order to feel included in the communications network.

Barriers to communication across the organization can include geographic dispersal and the compartmentalism of different departments and specialisms. Library organizations can have particular difficulties here. Library organizations are often geographically dispersed with a lack of communication between 'central' and the branches in public library systems; or between the 'main library' and the site libraries in some academic institutions. There is also sometimes a lack of communication between functional departments (lending, reference, bibliographic services, etc.).

Technology may well be able to help in breaking down some of these cross-organizational barriers. Electronic mail is a valuable hybrid which can have (like verbal communication) an interactive element and which can be (like written communication) precisely worded and formally recorded. Email networks enable staff to communicate frequently irrespective of geographic dispersal. A number of the 'integrated systems' (automating cataloguing, circulation control, acquisitions, serials control, etc.) in use in large UK libraries have the capability to support an Email network. It may be that Email will become a useful tool by which management can widen communication flow and increase participation in discussions and decisions within library organizations. Good communications are essential to a healthy organization and a contented workforce. As Anne Mathews emphasizes 'high morale and motivation stem from open communications'.[24]

There are a number of things which can be done – aside from exploring the potential of new technology – if managers wish to increase the effectiveness of organizational communications. One is simply for management to be aware of the need to review communications. The concept of the 'open door' (as in 'if you want to come and see me, my door is always open') illustrates the discrepancy which often exists between a manager's self-perception and the way in which that manager's style is perceived by other members of staff. The manager may think the door is open – but in practice the manager is often out of the office, or busy, and staff may feel inhibited about just 'popping in for a chat'.

A second strategy is to create an environment which encourages communication. This involves managers taking pains to *listen* more effectively – too often, meetings become a series of monologues rather than a dialogue or true discussion. It also involves creating a climate of trust. Staff will not offer their observations, opinions or information if that material is then used to exploit a situation, condemn an action, or gossip about an individual.

The third strategy is to create 'communication opportunities' within the organization. The use of temporary teams and matrix structures is valuable in this regard, as is a culture which supports the concept of 'management by wandering about'. Coffee (or tea) breaks and lunchtimes are also excellent opportunities for informal communications, as is the time-honoured tradition of 'a quick drink after work'. Some managers also see social events – Christmas parties, summer barbeques, charity sports events, etc. – as an important part of this process and act as a catalyst for such events.

Social events bring people together and can build a feeling of collective identity and 'team spirit'. They can help to break down barriers of status and formality and so can contribute to better interpersonal relations. They bring people out of their departments and into the organization as a whole thus encouraging integration and a sense of overall purpose. Above all, they can take people out of their job-roles and enable them to 'be themselves' as human beings.

Of course, this can be dangerous. The stereotype is of the 'office party', fuelled by alcohol and spiced with romance, which leads to embarrassment or calamity. When people are taken out of their usual roles the results are unpredictable. There may be people – particularly those who subscribe to a 'role' culture – who feel uncomfortable or out-of-place at such events, or who chose not to attend and then feel 'left out' of the group. But the potential for positive outcomes, in terms of team-building and networking, can outweigh the possibilities for discomfort or disaster.

An organization is a community, a mix of the mechanistic and the human, of technical and social systems. Formal structures co-exist with the 'hidden' organization of unwritten rules and alliances. Explicit contracts of employment co-exist with the implicit 'psychological contract' between each individual and the organization. Feelings, beliefs and shared values form the 'culture' which shapes attitudes and behaviour. This 'soft stuff' of people and their motivations is a key factor in determining the 'hard facts' of organizational performance. All are linked by formal and informal networks of communication.

Charles Handy writes of management style in terms of 'structuring' and 'supporting'. Clearly, managers need to give attention to both functions – and good communications are central to both. It is important to review organizational structures, bureaucratic processes, and formal channels of communication. It is equally important to be alive to the 'hidden' dimensions of individual psychology, organizational culture, and social networks. To promote a sense of community and nurture the social systems within the organization, it makes sense to provide opportunities for informal socializing outside the roles and restrictions of the organization itself.

References

1 A useful historical overview of the development of management theory in the context of library science is given in Robert D. Stueart and John Taylor Eastlick, *Library management*, 2nd ed., Littleton, Colorado, Libraries Unlimited Inc., 1981.

2 Douglas McGregor, *The human side of enterprise*, New York, McGraw-Hill, 1960.

3 Rensis Likert, *New patterns of management*, New York, McGraw-Hill, 1961.

4 Robert R. Blake and Jane S. Mouton, *The managerial grid*, Houston, Gulf Publishing, 1964.

5 Noragh Jones and Peter Jordan, *Staff management in library and information work*, 2nd edition, Gower, 1987, chapter 2. Stueart and Eastlick, *Library management*, Chapter 5.

6 Handy, *Understanding organizations*, p.97.

7 Peter Drucker, *Innovation and entrepreneurship*, Pan/Heinemann, 1986, pp.15 – 16.

8 Rosemary Stewart, *The reality of management*, 2nd edition, Heinemann, 1985, p.109.

9 Tom Lupton, *Management and the social sciences*, 3rd edition, Penguin, 1983, p.137.

10 See *Campus of the future: conference on information resources; Wingspread Conference Center, June 22 – 24, 1986*, Dublin, Ohio, OCLC, 1987.

11 See OAL, *School libraries: the foundations of the curriculum*, Library Information Series number 13, HMSO, 1984.

12 Sheila Ritchie (ed.), *Modern library practice*, p.85.

13 An emotively presented case study of local authority decentralization is given in Jeremy Seabrook, *The idea of neighbourhood: what local politics should be about*, Pluto, 1984.

14 Stueart and Eastlick, *Library management* (p.58f.), identify six methods – adding division by numbers, and by process or equipment. These

are used in specialized (non-library) situations, and so are not discussed here.

15 E. F. Schumacher, *Small is beautiful: a study of economics as if people mattered*, Blond and Briggs, 1973, p.58.
16 Tom Peters and Nancy Austin, *A passion for excellence: the leadership difference*, Fontana/Collins, 1986, p.210.
17 Rosemary Stewart, *The reality of management*, p.122.
18 Charles Handy, *Understanding organizations*, pp.186 – 96.
19 *Ibid.*, p.42.
20 *Ibid.*, p.196.
21 Thomas J. Peters and Robert H. Waterman, *In search of excellence: lessons from America's best-run companies*, New York, Harper and Row, 1982.
   Tom Peters and Nancy Austin, *A passion for excellence: the leadership difference*, Fontana/Collins, 1986.
   Walter Goldsmith and David Clutterbuck, *The winning streak: Britain's top companies reveal their formulas for success*, Penguin, 1985.
22 Kenneth Blanchard and Spenser Johnson, *The one minute manager*, Fontana/Collins, 1983.
23 Ken Jones, *Conflict and change in library organizations: people, power, and service*, Bingley, 1984, p.32.
24 Anne J. Mathews, *Communicate! A librarian's guide to interpersonal relations*, Chicago, ALA, 1983, p.59.

4 *The human dimension*

Introduction

An organization is only as good as the people who work in it.
The technical systems, hierarchical structures and bureaucratic
procedures set a framework for what is done within the
organization. How *well* it is done depends on people – the
'players' who put the systems and theories, the objectives and
strategies, into practice. The quality of organizational performance
depends on individual effort and, as Peters and Austin emphasize,[1]
excellence is a voluntary commitment. Getting people to make
that commitment involves finding out what makes them 'tick'
– what enthuses them and makes them 'feel good'.

Managers are dealing, not with a (depersonalized) 'workforce',
but with a collection of individual people. It is neither possible
nor desirable to treat those people as 'hired hands' – to focus
on the job-role while excluding the human being. An holistic view
is needed, seeing personality and role as an integrated whole.
People need to 'feel good' not just in relation to the job, but *about
themselves*. If personality and job-role are out of step, this will not
happen.

This is particularly important in a service organization like a
library, where staff are interacting constantly with customers,
frequently without any direct supervision or assistance from senior
librarians. In an office or factory it may well be possible to 'work
round' someone who is grouchy, or cynical, or depressive. But
attitude problems – whether rooted in the individual, personal
circumstances, or the work situation – are not permissible at
the point of customer service.

A manager, therefore, has to develop some insight into the
'psychological contract' of aspirations and expectations that each
individual brings to his or her work. This is one reason why 'spans

94

of control' (see Chapter 3) need to be structured with care. A manager can give detailed attention to only a limited number of staff.

Two points are important here. The first is that each individual psyche is different, and it is therefore not possible to make many generalizations about 'getting people to play' or helping people to 'feel good about themselves' – other than the basic principle that managers need to pay close attention to this area. Theories of leadership, motivation and 'human resource development' can provide a useful toolkit of indicators and possibilities, but how these are applied depends very much on individual circumstances.

The other point, taking an holistic view, is that an individual's 'psychological contract' with work will be affected by the role which work plays in that individual's overall life. Much management literature is written – and read – by people for whom work is profoundly important. But, for many people, work (in the sense of paid, organized work) does not assume such a large significance in their emotional and mental lives. They find key satisfactions outside the workplace. This is a particularly important point with regard to libraries. The 'counter staff' – that is, the library assistants working on the circulation desk, dealing with requests, and generally providing the front line of service to customers – are unlikely to be career-track librarians. Some may be students working to pay their way through their studies. Some may be working, perhaps part-time, to supplement the family income. Some may be volunteers with a strong personal commitment – but a clear sense of the point at which that commitment ends. Most will rank family or other 'outside' concerns above the job in their personal scale of values and priorities. This in no way denigrates their contribution to the library service; indeed in public libraries such staff have particular value, because of their local links with the customer community. Equally, there have always been career-track librarians with strong 'outside' interests and preoccupations – notably as writers. Again, this does not mean that they are any the less competent or conscientious – or even excellent – in the way they perform their job-related duties. But a manager with workaholic tendencies and unrealistic expectations may be disappointed to discover that not everyone responds with equal delight to a barrage of 'human resource development' strategies. The search for 'excellence' can be counter-productive if an overly enthusiastic manager does not recognize that commitment to organizational objectives always has its personal limits.

These general points – which concern, in essence, the need to respect each member of staff as an individual – must be borne in mind throughout any discussion of the issues raised in this chapter: workforce planning, staff development, leadership, motivation, and the 'institutionalism' that, at time, causes libraries to under-perform as organizations.

Workforce planning

Workforce planning can be described as an attempt to relate present human resources to future staffing needs. It combines a rational assessment of organizational requirements with the sort of 'people' considerations outlined above. The process of workforce planning[2] is, in theory, straightforward. The organization's objectives are translated into staffing requirements: the numbers of people and the skills needed. Each job is defined and analysed, and a specification is drawn up. This might include:

- function and purpose of the job
- degree of responsibility
  - for staff
  - for other assets
- degree of supervision received
- list of duties
- any special conditions (e.g. evening or weekend work; ability to drive)
- complexity of work
- element of creativity/thinking
- element of decision-making
- personal contacts (e.g. with customers)
- specific requirements (education, specialist qualifications, experience).

From the planning perspective, this process has considerable benefit. It enables the organization to identify, analyse and prepare for future changes in staffing structures (brought about, for example, by the introduction of new technology or new patterns of service provision) in a rational, planned way. It can help determine the grading of posts and the costing – in terms of staff – of service developments. It helps to identify training needs.

The challenge for management comes when the analysis of future staffing needs is set against the nature of existing staff resources. There may well be a discrepancy in numbers, or skills and attributes, or both. Resources are likely to be constrained, so that the relatively simple solution of recruiting additional staff is not always viable. At a time when jobs are scarce there is unlikely to be a high turnover of staff, so 'bringing in new people' to replace those who leave will not meet the pace of change required. Offering early retirement and voluntary redundancy schemes may help to create some movement, but these will only apply in particular circumstances. Compulsory redundancy and terminating employment are strategies to be used only in times of crisis and instances of misconduct or demonstrable incompetence.

Workforce planning can create conflict between the best interests of the organization and the best interests of existing staff. For example, some organizations have moved to fixed-term contracts (staff appointed for a defined period – say three years – rather than being given a 'permanent' contract) in order to retain a measure of control and flexibility at a time of constrained resources, rapid change and slow staff turnover. Some trade unions feel that this is not in the best interests of staff (less job security, more pressure to conform in order to win a contract renewal) and so they oppose the movement to fixed-term contracts. One of the difficult challenges for senior and middle management is to handle the potential conflict and confrontation that can result from the process of workforce planning.

Two other strategies are available as a means of implementing changes indicated by the workforce planning process. One is redeployment – moving people to other jobs within the organization. This needs to be negotiated with considerable sensitivity and support if a redeployment programme is not to cause resentment, low morale and the possibility of industrial action. The other is a comprehensive and continuous programme of staff training and development. This may not solve all the problems of discrepancy between organizational requirements and staffing resources – but it gives staff every opportunity to adapt to changing needs; and it demonstrates that management is

97

concerned not just with *structuring* the organization but also with *supporting* the people in it. The process of workforce planning must be supported by an adequate staff development programme.

Developing people

Margaret Slater has shown[3] that a library service usually has a dual perspective from the customer's viewpoint. It is viewed as a technical system – an organizational 'machine' – and also as a human, social network. Evidence for this duality emerges from user studies in which, for example, a respondent might be attracted to the library as a place but find the staff unhelpful; or might find the staff helpful and friendly but see the library itself as poorly stocked, shabbily furnished, etc. Slater's research (in the context of industrial and commercial libraries) suggests that negative customer perceptions relate more to the staff than the system.

Some of those negative comments may be a result of the way in which the service is organized or the level at which it is resourced (staff too busy to help; assistance too generalized and superficial; service only provides books and documents). Some may be intrinsic, related to the capabilities of an individual member of staff (ignorant and ill-educated; willing but not competent; lacks communicative and interpretative skills; misfit). But others suggest a lack of enthusiasm which might indicate a poor sense of group affiliation and team spirit (passive and apathetic; cold and aloof; casual attitude). A link can be drawn between customer perceptions and the quality of customer service, staff attitudes and performance, and the level of social affiliation and team spirit within the work group.

One reason for poor team spirit within the work group can be problems with 'the boss' – the manager of that group. Students on the degree course in Librarianship and Information Studies at Birmingham Polytechnic spend the third of their four years on work placement. As part of the 'debriefing' after this year of work experience, students discuss the experience of working with other people and the difficulties that can arise within the work group. Quite often, a lengthy checklist of negative comments about 'the boss' emerges:

● The absentee boss who is either 'always out at meetings' or 'hiding in the office' and who is therefore remote from the day-to-day reality of service delivery.

- The uncommunicative boss who does not share information with the staff and does not explain *why* – does not explain the purpose and value of things which the staff are asked or required to do.
- The 'burnt out' boss who doesn't seem to care much, whose career has stagnated, and who operates with a very *laissez-faire* management style.
- The incompetent boss who has been promoted to a level beyond his or her capabilities and simply cannot do the job required.
- The over-enthusiastic boss who has unrealistic expectations and sets impossible targets.
- The bandwagon boss who leaps, erratically, from one passing fashion to the next without ever following through or devising a coherent framework of objectives.
- The threatening boss who exercises power (by virtue of status and authority) but does not inspire trust.
- The over-burdened boss who has not learnt how to delegate work; who spends too much time on tasks which should be given to others and so does not have enough time to pay close attention to those matters which should be the boss's prime concern.

Two things are important here. One is that the students were talking, in the main, about their immediate line managers, not about senior management. Clearly, just as management can come relatively early in a librarian's career, so too can management failings. The other is that, in order to deal with these situations, it becomes important for staff to develop the skills of 'managing the boss'. This involves a mix of tact and assertiveness. Paradoxically, a poor boss can create team spirit – the comradeship that can develop in adversity – as the work group comes together in order to compensate for poor quality management.

An equally lengthy checklist emerges when discussing problems of working with peer colleagues or with those who are subordinate in the organizational hierarchy:

- Refusal to do something ('That's not my job' often linked to

the division between professional and non-professional status).
- Doing something grudgingly.
- Lack of commitment.
- Laziness (e.g. lack of thoroughness).
- 'Bolshie-ness' (i.e. a generally resentful and grumpy manner).
- Unwillingness to change.
- Absenteeism and bad time-keeping.
- A 'prima donna' attitude.
- People with poor interpersonal (communicating, socializing) skills.
- People who lack confidence in themselves.
- People who express boredom and/or frustration with work.
- Incompetence.

Like the 'boss' list, this is not a carefully researched checklist. It is not comprehensive and there is no attempt to gauge which types of difficulty might be more, or less, common. But it is indicative of the range of 'people' problems which can inhibit the growth of good team spirit and thwart attempts to provide a high standard of customer service. It is a range of problems which can apply at any level of the organizational hierarchy and so is pertinent to all levels of library manager – including the recently qualified librarian taking on a first-level management post with some responsibility for the work of a group of library assistants.

This may seem a dispiriting start to a section on 'developing people'. But, in reality, people cannot be 'developed' unless they are open and hospitable to the concept of development. Training programmes and development opportunities only have value if the participants truly participate. Success depends on individual commitment and motivation. The starting point for any discussion on development, therefore, has to be the obstacles – in terms of personal attitudes and characteristics – which need to be identified and dealt with before any staff development programme can succeed.

It may be that some of the 'people' problems mentioned above cannot be solved amicably in particular instances where a person has an inherently difficult or inappropriate personality. This stresses the importance of the recruitment and selection process in 'matching' people not just with jobs but also with particular work groups and organizational cultures. It also has to be accepted that there are some boring jobs to be done in libraries, as in any organization. There is very little that can be done to 'enrich' the job of bar-coding books, or filing issue slips, for example. What is important is that the work is organized so that no one person spends a disproportionate amount of time on one particularly tedious chore.

Job rotation (moving people around on a regular basis) is a valuable strategy for providing variety and also gives staff a wider knowledge of the library's systems and services. Manchester Polytechnic Library, for example, divides the day into four periods in the technical services department so that library assistants have a regular change of routine task.[4] Some public libraries rotate library assistants so that they move to a different branch library every six months. As well as providing variety, this is helpful when library assistants have to move around to provide temporary 'relief' cover for unplanned absences (sickness, etc.).

Job 'enrichment' is the concept of adding more challenging/rewarding tasks to the basic job. The matrix structures of team librarianship provide an example of this with individuals having some responsibility for particular stock areas and service functions as well as for a specific geographic territory. Subject specialism in academic libraries provides another example although, as Jones and Jordan point out,[5] constraints on staffing can mean that subject specialists spend a considerable amount of time on administrative and procedural work and relatively little time on the more 'enriched' aspects of subject specialization (user education, reader advisory work, collection development).

Fundamental to the process of 'developing people', then, are careful attention to recruitment and selection, and to staff deployment – the way that the work is organized and responsibilities allocated – and some understanding of the 'psychological contract' of individual staff. A further fundamental is a good communications network so that the manager has a thorough and current awareness both of people and of training/development opportunities; and so can match one to the other. The concept of MBWA (Management By Wandering About) is important here both in building up good interpersonal relations and also in identifying development opportunities.

The concepts of *training* and *development* overlap, although some distinctions can be drawn. *Training* implies a structured sequence of events (training courses, etc.) with clear objectives and outcomes which usually relate to the acquisition or improvement of skills.[6] *Development* is a much more 'open' concept, often with much less precise objectives and outcomes to do with attitude, awareness and maturity. Both should be a continuous process throughout working life (to keep up to date with new skills and knowledge and so maintain a 'fresh' approach to the job) and both are active processes. Individuals cannot be passive recipients of training or 'development' – there needs to be an active, personal involvement.

Both training and development can be stimulated and provided from a variety of sources:

- The individual who identifies a personal training or 'development' need and finds a way of meeting it (takes an evening course in computer studies, for example, as personal preparation for library automation; or joins the local committee of a professional group in order to get some experience of this kind of semi-formal meeting).
- The line manager who has a vital role to play in this area, identifying and anticipating the training and development needs of the staff in his or her span of control; and bringing opportunities to the attention of those staff.
- The organization as a whole which should have a policy and programme of staff training, and mechanisms for facilitating development.
- External bodies – educational establishments, training consultancies, professional bodies, etc. The plethora of professional associations and groups within librarianship all offer a programme of speakers, seminars, conferences, study schools, etc.; and also provide excellent opportunities for development through active involvement in their affairs.

Training can be linked to particular groups of staff or specific organizational objectives:

- Induction training of new staff. This is a particularly important area of training which needs careful planning. Beginning work in a new organization can be stressful and first impressions will be very deeply etched.

- Training for particular groups of staff; for example, newly-qualified librarians or staff who share a particular specialism like children's work.
- Training in particular areas of work (e.g. selecting stock, handling customer enquiries).
- Training to prepare for innovation; for example, to prepare staff for the implementation of a user education programme, or an automated issue system.

An important area of training with particular relevance to the concerns of this book is post-experience management training. This is valuable both on promotion to a job with supervisory responsibilities, and on promotion from departmental head to a senior management position that requires a view wider than that of one particular functional department. There is current concern, in the UK, about the nature and extent of management education and training. Libraries, like other organizations, need to consider the opportunities for staff training and development which are being offered in this expanding area.

Management training – like all other forms of training – can be organized in a variety of ways. It can be arranged to take place 'off the job', either by running in-house sessions or by using external agencies. It also takes place, continuously, on the job through supervised instruction and the process of doing the job itself.

Development is a less structured and more personalized process than training. It also has more to do with the needs of individuals rather than groups of staff. Rather than setting up 'development programmes' in the way that training programmes are set up, it is more a matter of creating or identifying and responding to development opportunities. These can take a variety of forms such as

- 'Deputizing' for, or acting as an assistant to, a more senior member of staff; or 'acting up' during a temporary vacancy (for example, during maternity leave, or in the period between a member of staff leaving and a successor arriving).
- Serving on committees, working parties, project teams, etc.
- Job exchanges and secondments.

- Attending courses and conferences. These can provide valuable personal and professional development on a general level – for example, through the social contacts made – as well as focussing on a particular area of work or concern.

These are all types of development which can be arranged, formally, on an organizational level. There are other types of development where the onus is more on the individual to take advantage of opportunities. Personal reading is an important part of professional development. The organization can support this by putting appropriate journals on circulation to staff, but it is up to each individual how much effort and attention is given to those journals when they arrive.

Professional associations provide major opportunities for personal, professional and managerial development. There are many such associations (national bodies, regional branches, specialist groupings, etc.), each of which is involved in formulating policy, planning professional meetings, producing publications and generally providing services to members and managing the association's affairs. Most of this work is done by librarians – in councils and committees, on working groups, and as individuals – working voluntarily in their free time. The benefits to those involved are great – in terms of heightened awareness, breadth of experience, and personal contacts. Such associations always welcome members who are willing to make a personal contribution of time and effort – and librarians who aspire to management and to being a 'professional' in the best sense of the word can gain enormous satisfaction from such involvement. Again, the onus is on the individual although the employing organization can be supportive by being reasonably flexible with regard to the time that this work requires, and by paying staff subscriptions to appropriate professional bodies.

Line managers have a very important role to play in relation to the development of staff for whom they are responsible. It is their responsibility to encourage and support staff in taking advantage of appropriate opportunities. It is also their responsibility to deal with what might be termed 're-entry' problems – that is, the frustrations which can be experienced by staff who return, invigorated, with expectations and aspirations raised, from a training course or development experience and who then find that in the mundane world of reality things can move a little more slowly than they might wish.

The line manager also plays a crucial role in helping staff to develop their ability to reflect on and learn from their experiences at work. This is particularly important in relation to 'crisis situations' when things get out of hand or a member of staff makes a mistake; for example, when staff have to deal with a 'difficult' customer. These difficult incidents can be viewed negatively; staff can be embarrassed, or annoyed, or upset by the memory. However, with sensitive handling and careful discussion, such incidents can become 'learning experiences' and so make a positive contribution to the development of the individual concerned. The other side of this coin is that good work should not be taken for granted and pass unnoticed. Thanking staff for work well done is courteous and helps to build confidence. It gives people the feeling of 'making a contribution' to the organization, and develops in them a sense of achievement.

Training covers technical/professional and sometimes certain managerial skills. Development covers a much wider range of professional, managerial and personal skills, attitudes and attributes. In relation to training, the role of the manager is relatively straightforward as provider or enabler. In relation to development, that role is more subtle and overlaps, in some instances, with the process of coaching, counselling and mentoring which is also an important part of 'developing people'.

The skills of coaching and counselling are sometimes difficult to acquire, but they can be learnt. Some people do have a personality which lends itself naturally to this approach but all managers can develop these skills which can contribute a tremendous amount to the level of social affiliation and team spirit generated within a work group.

From the manager's viewpoint a counselling session has five stages:

- Establishing rapport. Without open communications and a measure of trust, counselling cannot work constructively. This process of opening up communications and generating trust is something that a line manager should be working on continuously within the work group; again, Managing By Wandering About can help here. But however good and trusting communications are in general, there will still be a need, when counselling is taking place, to put the individual concerned at ease.

- Getting the other person's view. The emphasis here is on 'drawing out' the individual being counselled. Listening rather than talking, and asking 'open' and non-directive questions to widen and deepen discussion, rather than the manager 'jumping in' with comments and questions which narrow down the focus to a particular line of thought.
- Understanding the situation, and getting agreement on what that situation is. Both people discuss and analyse the situation until each is clear on the other's views and there is a consensus as to the specific elements of the situation.
- Discussing possible options and agreeing on actions.
- Summarizing these conclusions and ending the session.

Two important points should be made here. One is that the manager needs to prepare carefully for the session, thinking through all the possible ramifications of the situation. For example, if a relatively new member of staff is having difficulty, on occasions, in dealing with customers, the 'problem' may not simply lie with that person's attitude or capabilities. There may be weaknesses in training or communications, or the underlying 'culture' of the work group may not have conveyed itself to the new member of staff. Some elements in the situation may reflect on the manager doing the counselling, and not just on the individual being counselled. The second point is the importance of agreeing on actions (ideally, with timescales) and then following up those promises by putting them into effect. Trust, commitment and a sense of feeling valued will soon be replaced by corrosive cynicism if a manager's counselling is all fine words, but no back-up action.

The process of coaching and counselling can evolve, on occasions, into 'mentoring' – a strong one-to-one relationship between someone relatively new and inexperienced and someone with depth of experience and understanding. The relationship is mutually beneficial. In simple terms, innocence can learn from the wisdom of experience, and experience can gain new insights from the fresh eyes of innocence. Just as a mentor can be helpful to a young librarian who aspires to climb the management ladder, so it is important for senior managers to make themselves available, in a mentoring capacity, to help that generation of librarians who will ultimately succeed them.

Coaching, counselling and mentoring are often informal processes. They happen because of managers' attitudes and actions, not because there is any formal programme. However, some organizations do attempt to systematize them. Counselling is sometimes built into formal programmes of staff training and development, with line managers given training in counselling skills; and at Barnet College in London all new staff are assigned to a mentor.[7]

A more common way of formalizing this type of process is through a scheme of staff appraisal. There is some ambivalence about such schemes. Do they work in a positive and supportive way to meet organizational objectives – by building personal confidence and a sense of achievement, setting realistic and agreed targets, providing constructive feedback, helping shape the way in which resources are deployed? Or are they judgemental and critical – a means of applying pressure to individual staff? John Cowley comments[8] that the assessment of individual performance is a highly emotive subject and can seriously damage morale if badly handled. He stresses the importance of:

- careful negotiations between management, staff, and unions in setting up such a scheme.
- training in appraisal for line managers who are to operate the scheme.
- regular feedback on performance rather than 'hoarding' criticism or praise until the annual review takes place.
- open-ness (with, for example, individuals having access to documented views on their performance).
- encouragement for the process of self-appraisal within the context of organizational objectives.

Much depends on a healthy organizational culture and a supportive management style. The contrast has already been made between a *structuring* and a *supportive* culture. The former views staff as 'human resources' (in a somewhat depersonalized way) and provides a framework for individual action which can be perceived as essentially repressive. The latter views staff as

107

'resourceful humans' and the framework for individual action is seen and discussed as liberating; what *can* rather than what *cannot* be done. This is a caricature contrast and, in reality, organizational life will be a mix of both styles. But an appraisal scheme is likely to be viewed more positively if the prevailing style tends to be supportive and liberating rather than being based on structures and strictures.

The core of the scheme is usually an annual 'appraisal interview' or 'development discussion' between each employee and his or her line manager. This is a one-on-one confidential discussion, preferably carried out on 'neutral' territory, in a relatively informal manner, and without interruptions. All staff in the organization should be appraised in this way, with the chief executive appraised by a group of senior members of the governing body – the board of directors, local council, university senate or whatever. The discussion will cover all aspects of work activity during the previous year and in the year to come. From the organizational perspective the aims of the discussion are

- to bring together personal and organizational objectives in a way which builds a strong individual commitment and a healthy psychological contract.
- to clarify the purpose and objectives of a particular job in relation to those for the department or organization as a whole.
- to discuss and clarify areas of success and difficulty in the job.
- to agree on specific steps to be taken in order to meet the training and development needs of the individual being appraised.

From the perspective of the individual being appraised there are additional (but complementary) aims:

- to provide feedback on performance.
- to provide an opportunity to discuss career progress and prospects.
- to exchange ideas on the nature of the job being done.

In those organizations where pay is related to performance, a further aim is added: determining the level of that performance-related element.

As with the less formal counselling process, it is important that individuals being appraised be given every opportunity to express their viewpoints and wishes – including putting forward proposals for their own development and job enrichment.

The outcome of the discussion will be an 'action plan' negotiated and agreed by both parties which details:

- the end results required
- target dates by which those results are to be achieved
- actions required (and by whom they are to be done).

This 'action plan' can then form the basis for an ongoing process of appraisal (for example when one of the target dates is reached) and also provide the starting point for the next year's formal discussion.

The process of appraisal can be seen partly in terms of 'developing people' and partly in terms of the manager's 'control' function in that it monitors performance in relation to established targets.

Schemes differ in the amount of documentation attached to them. In some, for example, both parties complete preparatory documents before the discussion to highlight points they wish discussed. In others, a (countersigned) document is produced which forms an agreed summary of the discussion itself. What is important, in all schemes, is that the 'action plan' be documented so that it can be referred to, as an objective record, as the year progresses.[9]

As staff become more experienced, both at work and with the appraisal scheme, the balance of the discussion can alter from a situation where the manager is providing a series of 'prompts' to a situation where the individual being appraised is articulating a process of self-assessment. A vital aspect of 'developing people' is stimulating and supporting the ability of individuals to diagnose and reflect on their own work experience. This is at the heart of Peter Drucker's concept[10] of 'management by objectives *and self-control*' (my italics) and also lies behind the concept of the Professional Development Report – the Report on which the UK Library Association assesses an individual member's fitness to be added to the Register of Chartered Librarians. Perhaps the most crucial thing that is looked for in such a report is the individual's ability to consider and analyse their own work experience in terms of personal, professional and managerial development.

As with all the strategies mentioned in this section, staff appraisal – if conducted in the right spirit – leads not just to improved job performance but also to heightened personal morale. It can have the 'Hawthorne effect' of making people feel valued and 'special'. Rosemary Stewart suggests[11] that people enjoy their work – and thus, the implication is, work better – when they become part of a social group 'in which they are important as a person'. The processes of training, development, coaching and counselling, mentoring, appraisal, are all ways in which the manager can show, with actions as well as words, that the people in the work group are important and valued as individual human beings. People, like plants, will grow to their full potential only when nurtured.

Leadership and motivation

Much of the previous section touched on issues of *motivation* and *leadership*. The two are closely interlinked, indeed the ability to inspire and motivate staff is generally held to be one of those exceptional qualities which transforms a *manager* into a *leader*. People work well, with enthusiasm and 'excellence', when they feel good about themselves, their job, and their contribution towards the overall purpose of the organization. The study of *motivation* could be described as the study of what – in a work context – makes people 'feel good'.

Early theories of motivation (for example the 'hierarchy of needs' developed by Abraham Maslow in the 1950s) included basic physiological needs (the 'life support systems' of food, water, clothing, shelter, sleep, etc.) and also the need for security – the need to know that these 'life support systems' are not threatened and are likely to continue. In the work context this includes feelings of job security and organizational stability.[12] The next level in Maslow's hierarchy focusses on the need for social affiliation – the feeling of belonging to a group, of acceptance and friendliness and good team spirit. Later theorists (the first being Frederick Herzberg) have suggested that these basic needs cease to act as motivators once they have been satisfied. They are a necessary foundation – and their absence causes loss of morale – but they do not, in themselves, inspire people to exceptional efforts. Herzberg suggests that positive motivating factors correspond with the two highest levels of Maslow's hierarchy:

- Esteem: recognition, status and respect from others.
- Self-fulfilment: career accomplishment and personal growth; expertise and responsibility; a sense of realizing one's full potential.

What connects these two levels is the need for achievement: either recognized by others (esteem) or felt oneself (self-fulfilment). People who have developed this need for achievement share a number of characteristics:

- They are 'self-starters' who respond to challenges, seek autonomy, and wish to take personal responsibility for outcomes.
- They set achievement goals for themselves and are happy to take calculated risks.
- They have a strong need for feedback on performance (to reinforce the sense of achievement).
- They have well-developed skills in planning (setting objectives) and organizing (determining strategies by which those objectives can be achieved).

Research (by David McClelland and others) suggests that there is a link between good organizational performance and staff with a strong need for achievement. McClelland also suggests that this need can be developed in individuals. This is an important point because it links together motivation theories based on the *needs* which stimulate behaviour and those which focus on the *processes* which condition behaviour. 'Expectancy theory', for example, suggests that the motivation to act in a certain way depends on perceptions regarding the likely outcome of the action. Faced with a number of options for action, a decision might be based on

- relative value of desired outcome.
- relative probability of achieving desired outcome.
- relative effort required.

If one option will produce a high-value outcome, with a high probability of achieving that outcome, for relatively little effort – then the motivation to act will be strong. But if the effort required is great and the probability of achieving the outcome is low – then motivation will be much weaker.

Perceptions and expectations regarding value, probability and effort will be based on previous experiences within the organization. If previous efforts have been rebuffed (the classic concept of 'hitting one's head against a brick wall'), then motivation to try something similar will lessen. This expectancy theory is represented diagrammatically in Figure 8.

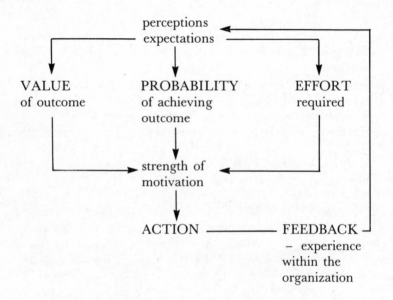

Figure 8: Expectancy theory: motivation to act depends on perception of the likely outcome of the action

Centralized management processes and bureaucratic systems do not encourage the conditions which help to nurture an individual's sense of achievement. Instead, they can become the 'brick wall' by which achievement-orientation can be rebuffed and destroyed. One of the advantages of building 'smallness' into large organizations (see Chapter 3) is that it then becomes possible to offer opportunities for responsibility and achievement at all levels of the organizational structure. Some small information units for example – because of their small span of control (and consequent care for individuals), open communications, and delegation of responsibility – help to develop in individuals the need for achievement. Small, one-person libraries can provide precisely the challenge that achievement-oriented librarians find rewarding.

Mark Shields makes the point[13] that some people do not necessarily seek responsibility and a sense of achievement through work. There are those who take satisfaction from the social relationships rather than the work itself, and those who work purely for economic reward. Shields comments that 'not everyone wishes to self-actualise at work' and suggests that 'lower order' needs (pay, working conditions) cannot be ignored. Shields also emphasizes the importance of job design and work organization,[14] linking motivation with such concepts as:

- extent of opportunities to use valued skills.
- extent to which the job produces a visible and meaningful outcome.
- extent to which the job is seen as significant in terms of its impact on other people.
- extent to which individuals have autonomy and discretion and so can feel responsible for the results of their work.

From the management perspective, motivation is concerned with bringing together organizational objectives and individual aspirations – generating and maintaining commitment through the 'psychological contract'. A number of factors can be identified which contribute to the evolution of this positive frame of mind. One is job design and the considerations outlined above. This leads on to two other factors:

- A sense of involvement and 'ownership'. This can be stimulated by open communications, and a democratized and participative management style in which power is shared. A good example of this is the concept of 'quality circles' (first used in Japanese manufacturing plants) by which small groups meet regularly to share and solve job-related problems. This process has the dual value of generating team spirit as well as creating a sense of ownership and responsibility for the job – while the outcomes of such meetings can help to solve problems and improve performance.

- A sense of being supported as workers and valued as individuals. Important here are the processes discussed in the previous section – of training and development, counselling and appraisal. Also important is recognition (emphasized in Chapter 3) of the 'social' side of work.

These factors are to do partly with organizational structure, and partly with management style. There is general agreement amongst management writers that a participative style of management increases job satisfaction amongst the staff, and that this, in turn, increases productivity and the quality of staff performance.

Libraries do not always match up well when considered with these factors in mind. The division between professional and non-professional staff (or, in universities, between staff on 'academic related' grades and the rest of the library staff) can obstruct open communications, quality circles and a sense of 'ownership'; as can other hierarchical and lateral (e.g. geographic or departmental) barriers. Inadequate communications within the organization is often one of the major 'grumbles' of discontented library staff. In addition, there is evidence that some libraries – at least, in the UK – pay insufficient attention to training[15] and this may be indicative of a management style which does not give a high priority to the need to support and develop staff.

The ability to motivate is a key element in the concept of *leadership*. Sir Kenneth Corfield, Chairman of Standard Telephones and Cables, has described a leader as someone who can 'unleash the aspirations' of staff.[16] 'Unleashing aspirations' suggests a structure which devolves responsibility and provides opportunities for achievement, and a culture which is liberating rather than repressive. It suggests a process of development, coaching/counselling and supportive appraisal. It also suggests a clear sense of mission and an inspiring vision.

Chris Bonington, top mountaineer and successful organizer of major climbing expeditions, defines the job of a leader in a way which echoes the classic management cycle: define task, plan schedule, assess team, explain roles, discuss detail, monitor progress, support efforts, evaluate results, debrief.[17] What is significant is the way Bonington expresses that cycle in terms which focus on the human dimension – working with and through a team of people. Bonington, like other commentators, defines the nature of leadership in terms of three key functions:

- achieving the task
- building team-spirit
- motivating individuals.

Fundamental to this is a shaping and inspiring vision – in Bonington's case, for example, an ascent of Everest – which gives direction and inspires commitment. The leader constantly reinforces that vision through communication and by action. It follows, therefore, that the leader must be highly visible.

The leader must also be flexible in terms of the style he or she choses to adopt in any particular situation. A checklist of contrasting management styles was given in Chapter 1. These, essentially, form a continuum from an autocratic, directive, structuring approach to one that is participative, democratic and supportive – the continuum as expressed in Chapter 3 through Likert's four types of management style: authoritative (exploitative or benevolent); consultative; participative. Victor Vroom has shown[18] how this continuum works in relation to the process of decision-making

- you make the decision yourself, using information available to you at the time.
- you obtain information from your subordinates, then make the decision yourself.
- you share the problem with subordinates individually, getting their ideas without bringing them together as a group. Then you make the decision.
- you share the problem with your subordinates as a group, collectively obtaining their ideas. Then you make the decision.
- you share the problem as a group, collectively evaluating solutions and attempting to reach a consensus agreement. Your

role is to chair the group and you will support and implement the group's decision.

There are a number of variables which will determine what style is used on what occasion. Much has been written, for example, on the relationship between management style and national characteristics – the German emphasis on 'technik', the British concern for the socio-political dimension, the 'go for it' attitude of Americans, the paternalism of Japanese companies, and so on.[19]

A certain amount has been written on the sensitive subject of gender and management style – on what might be termed the distinction between a 'macho' and a 'midwife' approach. The former – gung-ho, task and results orientated – style can be equated to the 'American' style of management. The latter – based on consensus, personal support, and team-building – might be equated to aspects of the 'Japanese' approach.

The personal characteristics of an individual leader are obviously important in determining a style with which he or she feels comfortable; so too are the characteristics and experience of the other team members. The characteristics of the particular situation – the organizational context, the nature of the problem, the time available to make a decision, etc. – also form an important set of variables.[20] John Cowley sums up the situation:[21]

> Modern personnel management as viewed through contingency theory will consist of a continuum of action and style of operation which will allow and justify everything from swift, executive action to painstaking consultation and extensive delegation depending on the circumstances prevailing at any one time.

There is ambiguity here. Managers should be capable of flexibility in the styles they choose to adopt. But managers should also have integrity. A style that is 'put on' will soon be detected – and derided – by staff. The continuum of possible styles is conditioned, for individual managers, by those approaches which fit naturally with their personality and character.

Whatever style is chosen, however, it is clear that hierarchical status alone does not confer the qualities of 'leadership' – any more than hierarchical authority alone can inspire motivation.

A person's influence comes partly from their position in the organization – but also from their personality. Rosemary Stewart makes two important points which enlarge on this.[22] One is that, in order to achieve tasks, managers in general (and perhaps leaders in particular) spend a lot of time with people who are not their subordinates. They may be from other departments within the organization or staff of other organizations (suppliers, for example). The traditional boss-subordinate hierarchy is irrelevant to these 'trading relations' which are based on mutual benefit and cooperation. The other is that the nature of boss-subordinate relations is changing as social characteristics change. The age of deference-to-authority for its own sake is over. Better education and more independence mean that people expect to be *consulted* rather than *told* what to do.

Motivation and leadership, then, are intertwined. They focus on a vision which shapes direction and inspires commitment. They focus on structures and styles which promote good communications and the sense that individuals are making a positive and valuable contribution to the organization, and which give individuals an opportunity to develop, take responsibility, and experience a sense of achievement. They focus on people, processes and tasks – not hierarchies and institutions.

Institutional barriers
A library can be described as an 'institution' in three ways

- Physical: the library as a building.
- Organizational: the library as a bureaucracy.
- Attitudinal: as reflected by the 'mind set' projected by the profession's establishment.

Each of these levels of institutionalism can act as a barrier to effective service delivery. The building itself, the rules and regulations involved in using the library, the traditionally subordinate/dependent relationship between 'client' and 'professional' – all can inhibit use of the library service.

'De-institutionalism' is concerned to break down these barriers. It is reflected in the 'deschooling' and 'deprofessionalism' philosophy of writers like Ivan Illich, and in the decentralization and neighbourhood-control movement in local government reflected, in the UK, by books like Jeremy Seabrook's *The idea of neighbourhood*.[23] It is also reflected, in the USA, by the 'mainstreaming' movement to bring the benefits of full citizenship to people with physical and mental disability.[24] Essentially, 'deinstitutionalism' promotes the idea of a service growing organically from within a community rather than being imposed from outside, and of a community taking control of its own development. This is achieved in three stages:

- giving the customer community direct access to resources.
- enabling the customer community to participate in providing and creating service.
- facilitating community control of resources and decision-making.

In library service both in the UK and the USA there has been some movement towards the first objective of providing community access to service. This is reflected in three ways:

- recognition that the library building itself can produce physical and psychological barriers, so that 'the first priority of a mainstreamed library is a barrier-free physical plant'.[25]
- attempts to take library service out of the library building ('outreach' etc.).
- organizational restructuring to reflect a more customer-orientated approach (community teams in public libraries, subject specialists in academic libraries, etc.).

But there are still attitudinal barriers which can prevent the library service from reaching its full potential to serve the customer community. Consider these three paradoxes of UK librarianship:

- The majority of library workers do not have professional qualifications; yet very few of these so-called 'non-professionals' are members of the Library Association.
- The majority of library workers are women; yet very few women hold senior management posts within libraries.
- Britain is a multicultural society and many public libraries have a policy of service delivery which explicitly states this; yet there are very few professional librarians in the UK from minority ethnic groups.

118

This section considers each of these three paradoxes in turn. What is meant by a 'professional' approach? The answer – conscientious, committed, concerned – focusses on *attitude*, not *status*. Yet the rigid demarcation which exists in UK librarianship between 'professional' and 'non-professional' is based on elitism and status-consciousness. This is reflected in the insulting terminology used (*non*-professional) and reinforced by a system of professional education which makes it very difficult for library assistants to become qualified librarians. The result is a 'them and us' situation within the UK library service which is not, perhaps, paralleled in other countries. A number of studies of 'non-professional' staff in British libraries have found that a major cause of dissatisfaction amongst library assistants is their relationship with the professionally qualified staff and vice-versa.[26]

From the viewpoint of a potential library assistant, the prospects for job satisfaction and career development look poor. Low status (often reflected in a relatively low salary grade) and a routine-based job; little opportunity for job enrichment (because 'non-professionals' are rarely involved in 'professional' discussions or activities) or for career progression, because of the unhelpful education/qualification system. It is no wonder that some libraries find it hard to attract library assistants of adequate calibre – or experience a high turnover of 'non-professional' staff.

In the USA and other countries these divisions are less distinct because of the existence of a 'para-professional' level of library worker and because of wider access to professional education through part-time study and open learning methods. In the past this was also true in the UK – when librarians qualified by part-time study and the Association of Assistant Librarians existed to support those library workers who were in the process of qualifying in this way. The drive to give librarianship the status of a 'graduate profession' has had the unfortunate side-effect of excluding 'non-professionals' from 'the profession' itself.

However, for most library assistants, access to professional education is not the issue; they have no particular desire to become 'professionals'. Nor is the nature of the work a cause of dissatisfaction. The satisfactions in the job are social/human rather than task-related. They come from good interpersonal relations with others in the work group, and from dealing on a personal level with library customers. The problems lie more in the organizational context: the division between 'professional' and 'non-professional' tasks; the nature of the supervision received; and the perceived attitudes of library management.[27]

Library assistants are devalued in the UK by the common terminology of 'the profession'. They are devalued within libraries by their low hierarchical status and their effective exclusion from the (professional/managerial) process of communication and decision-making. That they are devalued within the professional establishment is evidenced by the inappropriate education/qualification system and the lack of expressed concern for their interests reflected by bodies like the Library Association – although there is an encouraging move by the LA to focus more explicitly on the needs of 'para-professionals'.[28] Yet according to the 1981 Department of Education and Science (DES) census,[29] some 67% of the library/information workforce in the UK – some 34,800 people – are not qualified librarians; and these staff are likely to be (much more than 'professional' librarians) in the front line of direct service delivery. For the customer, the library service is personified – in the main – by the library assistant.

That same DES census indicates that 80 per cent of those non-qualified staff are women, and that 59% of professional staff are also women. Yet according to research carried out by Sheila Ritchie[30] in the late 1970s, women occupied only 27.5% of senior posts (graded Principal Officer or above) in UK public libraries. More recent UK data gathered by Gillian Burrington shows that in 1984, of 108 public library chief officer posts, only six were held by women.

Burrington's careful and revealing research study[31] relates this discrepancy to the wider culture of British society which subordinates women to men through an institutionalized status system whereby men are accorded greater prestige; and which perceives women as less interested in career development than men. It might be added, from the perspective of this book, that this institutionalized status system also perceives the stereotypical qualities attributed to men (dynamism, aggression, decisiveness) as appropriate for management and 'the professions'.

Burrington notes that women are less active and visible than men in 'the profession' as illustrated by articles in the professional press, membership of councils and committees, speakers and questioners at professional meetings and conferences. This has had the effect of reinforcing the male-dominated status quo – women's voices are not heard, topics of importance to women are not aired, and there are few women as role models to encourage other women to come forward. Burrington suggests that women need to make a positive effort to demonstrate their career commitment by involving themselves more actively in these arenas, by making themselves more visible, by actively seeking promotion, by creating training/development opportunities (for example, training in assertiveness), and by 'networking' – building up a web of useful and supportive personal contacts.

What is significant is the waste of management talent that results from this situation. There may be some truth in the gender stereotype which sees men as more aggressive/competitive and women as more caring/nurturing. The irony is that it is precisely those qualities of caring and nurturing which contribute to team-building and the sort of supportive culture which helps people 'feel good' about their work. In order to seek achievement in library management – or any area of management – women do not need to emulate the styles and strategies of men. Rather, male managers may have something to learn from the supportive and nurturing qualities which are, stereotypically, attributed to women.

While women are attracted into librarianship but are not yet adequately represented in library management, it would seem – at least, in the UK – that people from minority ethnic groups are not particularly keen to enter librarianship at all. Without research, possible reasons for this can only be speculative but they might include:

- The educational attainment needed in order to qualify as a librarian; many young people from minority ethnic groups find it difficult to realize their full educational potential in a British school system where the curriculum and assessment processes still reflect a single cultural perspective.
- Perceptions of librarianship as part of the British establishment (of government, the professions, etc.); perceptions of institutional racism within that establishment.
- Lack of role models within UK librarianship.
- Library service which reflects a single cultural perspective: in the way that classification schemes (as reflected in shelf

arrangement) can marginalize minority cultures; and in the way that 'services to ethnic minorities' are not incorporated into the mainstream of service provision in terms of either funding or staffing.

● Curricula within professional education which reinforce the status quo and do not address issues of racism and multiculturalism.

There is some evidence of concern about these issues within UK librarianship. In 1986, the Association of Assistant Librarians produced and publicized an Anti-Racist Statement and an Equal Opportunities Policy Statement.[32]

The UK Library Association itself has produced two policy statements, one (in 1985) on *Library and information services for our multicultural society*, the other (in 1986) on *The recruitment and training of library and information workers of ethnic minority background*. But policies take time to filter through into general practice. Any increase in recruitment of people from minority ethnic groups into librarianship today will take some years before these people become visible in leadership positions within the profession and begin to operate as role models, encouraging others to emulate them.

If libraries in the UK are to gain the advantage of a richer and more representative ethnic mix – and take advantage of the management talent in women library workers – and attract and keep high-quality library assistants – then the institutional establishment of librarianship needs to do something more than issue policy statements, useful though these are as a means of focussing attention on key issues.

That institutional establishment is represented by:

● the Council, committees and secretariat of professional bodies like the Library Association.
● the infrastructure of professional committees, meetings and networks that exists at local, regional and national (Library and Information Services Councils) levels.
● the management hierarchies of individual library services.

It is predominantly male, white and middle-class; and almost exclusively 'professional'. To create a single community of library workers where entry qualifications and gender are no barrier to progress and which reflects the ethnic mix of the customer community – and to 'unleash the aspirations' of those workers – that establishment needs to consider programmes of what Americans might term 'affirmative action'. When attending a conference in the USA,[33] it was encouraging to see a balance of men and women amongst the principal speakers and to hear, in discussion with a black delegate, that there is no feeling of institutional racism within American librarianship. But of 50-plus conference delegates, only two were black; and of 19 platform participants, only five were women. A survey of students enrolled in MLS programmes in the USA in 1988 revealed[34] that 93.7% were white, 80.9% were female, only 6.4% held science degrees – and that, although librarianship has changed considerably over the past 30 years, the background of librarianship students has not changed in any significant way. 'Affirmative action' may have progressed more strongly in the USA than in the UK, but in both countries there is some way to go before racial and sexual equality are fully reflected in leadership positions within the librarianship community.

Why do some libraries under-perform?

Customers perceive library services as a duality: a set of technical systems and a social system of human interactions. Discussions of performance measurement in libraries tend to focus on technical systems, while – as Margaret Slater has pointed out – negative comments from the customer community tend to focus on the social system, on the staff.

Performance measurement in libraries will be discussed in Chapter 6 when looking at the manager's 'control' function. But it is useful, at this point, to pull together those suggestions regarding performance which relate to the human/social dimension. Three general criticisms recur in the literature of librarianship:

- that the primary focus of librarians is on internal processes and materials.
- that the needs and perceptions of customers are consistently disregarded.
- that librarianship lacks leadership.

This chapter has identified a range of more explicit reasons which might help to explain why libraries are sometimes seen as organizations which under-perform:

- Organizational structures and value systems (as reflected in salary and status) take professional staff away from the front line of customer service.
- Front-line staff (library assistants) are devalued as *non-*professionals. For customers, the library service is personified by library assistants, but library organizations and the librarianship profession treats them with
  - low status and pay
  - routine-based jobs
  - little job enrichment
  - exclusion from communication and decision-making processes
  - poor career prospects
  - exclusion from 'professional' concerns.
- The management talents of the majority of library workers (i.e. women) are not fully used.
- Librarianship does not attract an ethnic mix which reflects the changing and multicultural nature of society.
- Library management is, in some cases, characterized by status-conscious hierarchies, centralized decision-making processes, bureaucratic systems and communications barriers.
- There is inadequate provision of in-service training and development opportunities for library staff. Research in the UK public library sector has shown that most library authorities allocate only a very small amount of resourcing (in terms of money and time) to training. One result of this is that librarians who find themselves, at a fairly early stage of their career, with some management responsibility are not always supported by organizational programmes for management training and development. The quality of line management is particularly crucial in libraries where service is, in the main, decentralized and delivered through small units and work groups. There is some, admittedly anecdotal, evidence to suggest that the effectiveness of these work groups is being damaged by problems with 'the boss', that is, the line manager.

Libraries, like other organizations, employ *techniques* of staff deployment and 'personnel management'. But those techniques – of job rotation, for example, or staff appraisal – need to be firmly based in an appropriate organizational *culture* and management *style*. This chapter has suggested that high-quality performance can result if that culture is supportive and liberating rather than structuring and repressive. To make people 'feel good' about themselves and their work, it is necessary to

- encourage an atmosphere conducive to the development of good social relations within the work group;
- stimulate and satisfy a sense of achievement;
- create feelings of involvement, responsibility, and 'ownership';
- generate a belief that people are supported in their work and valued as individuals.

Clearly senior management must be careful not to undermine middle management by 'leapfrogging' them and discussing policy directly with junior staff. But a distinction can be drawn between formal meetings (for policy formulation and decision-making) and less formal communications to exchange information and share views. It is possible to have open communications without damaging the formal chain of command. As John Cowley writes:[35]

It may be that firmly directed, non-consultative methods are still needed in crisis situations when time-scales are short and resources scarce, but, in general, the planning and direction of library teams requires a recognition of the value of member participation. The situation in the modern library is such that expertise, creativity, intelligent and constructive thought, and qualities of leadership can be found at all levels.

There are institutional barriers in libraries, and within the profession of librarianship, which can work against open communications, participation, and feelings of involvement and achievement – and so can prevent staff from 'feeling good' and working well. A major challenge for managers at all levels within librarianship is to shift the focus away from institutions and hierarchies and towards people and tasks; to motivate individuals and build team spirit; and to create structures and cultures by which people can satisfy personal aspirations in achieving organizational objectives.

References

1 Peters and Austin, *A passion for excellence*, p.210.
2 Workforce planning and a number of the other topics discussed in this chapter are described in detail in Noragh Jones and Peter Jordan, *Staff management in library and information work*, 2nd edition, Gower, 1987. Robert Stueart and John Eastlick, *Library management*, 2nd edition, Littleton, Colorado, Libraries Unlimited Inc., 1981, also includes useful sections on staffing and directing.
3 Margaret Slater, *Non-use of library-information resources at the workplace*, Aslib, 1984.
4 Reported in Jones and Jordan, *Staff management*, pp.73 – 4.
5 *Ibid.*, p.75.
6 An excellent overview of library training is provided by Sheila D. Creth, *Effective on-the-job training: developing human resources*, Chicago, ALA, 1986.
7 John Skitt, 'Setting up a staff development scheme: staff appraisal and training needs' in *Management issues in academic libraries*, ed. Tim Lomas, Rossendale, 1986, pp.67 – 72.
8 John Cowley, *Personnel management in libraries*, Bingley, 1982, pp.71 – 2.
9 Examples of appraisal schemes used in libraries are given in Jones and Jordan, *Staff management*, p.182f. Employee performance evaluation is also discussed in Stueart and Eastlick, *Library management*, p.97f.
10 Peter Drucker, *The practice of management*, p.133.
11 Rosemary Stewart, *The reality of management*, p.117.
12 Many management textbooks outline the various motivation theories. Charles Handy's *Understanding organizations* has a valuable discussion of this topic, while Jones and Jordan, *Staff management* and Stueart and Eastlick, *Library management*, relate motivation theory to library practice. Also useful is Mark Shields, *Work and motivation in academic libraries*, Bradford, MCB University Press, 1988.
13 Shields, *Work and motivation in academic libraries*, pp.29 – 30.
14 *Ibid.*, p.8.
15 Jean Bird, *In-service training in public library authorities*, LA, 1986.
16 Quoted in Goldsmith and Clutterbuck, *The winning streak*, p.26.
17 Chris Bonington, 'Getting to the top', *The Sunday Times*, 31 July 1988.
18 Vroom's ideas are presented in D. S. Pugh, D. J. Hickson and C. R. Hinings, *Writers on organizations*, 3rd edition, Penguin, 1983, pp.119 – 24.

19 There is some discussion of this in Peter Lawrence, *Management in action*, Routledge and Kegan Paul, 1984.

20 Rosemary Stewart, *The reality of management*, pp.68 – 9, summarizes a classic article on 'How to choose a leadership pattern' by Tannenbaum and Schmidt which usefully reviews the characteristics of managers, subordinates, and situations.

21 John Cowley, *Personnel management in libraries*, p.23.

22 Rosemary Stewart, *The reality of management*, p.201.

23 Jeremy Seabrook, *The idea of neighbourhood*, Pluto, 1984.

24 Barbara H. Baskin and Karen H. Harris, *The mainstreamed library: issues, ideas, innovations*, Chicago, ALA, 1982.

25 *Ibid.*, p.1.

26 David Baker, *What about the workers?* AAL, 1986.

27 Norman Russell, 'Professional and non-professional in libraries', *Journal of librarianship*, October 1985.

28 The *Library Association record* for August 1988 (p.434) announced the Library Association's intention to set up a category of 'para-professional' membership.

29 Department of Education and Science, *Census of staff in librarianship and information work in the UK, 1981*, OAL, 1982.

30 Sheila Ritchie, '2,000 to 1: a sex odyssey', *Assistant librarian*, **72**, (3), March 1979, pp.38 – 41.

31 Gillian Burrington, *Equal opportunities in librarianship? Gender and career aspirations*, LA, 1987.

32 Reported in *Assistant librarian*, March 1986.

33 *The future of the public library: conference proceedings, OCLC, Dublin, Ohio, March 20 – 22, 1988*, Dublin, Ohio, OCLC, 1988.

34 William E. Moen and Kathleen M. Heim, 'The class of 1988: librarians for the new millenium', *American libraries*, November 1988, **19**, (10), p.858f.

35 John Cowley, *Personnel management in libraries*, p.15.

5 Technology: a catalyst for change

Into the 'information age'

The concept of the 'post-industrial' society is now commonplace in scientific, sociological, and economic thinking.[1] After the agricultural age (with power and wealth based on land and cultivation), and the industrial age (based on capital and manufacturing), comes the 'information age' – with power and wealth based on the control and communication of knowledge. The emergence of this new age is characterized by:

- changes in the structure of the workforce; less emphasis on manufacturing industries and more on service and 'knowledge' industries;
- recognition of information as a key resource for economic growth;
- evolution of 'information management' – organizations becoming aware of the need to manage information in the planned way that they manage other key resources.

The 'engine' to stimulate and drive each of these three ages has been technology – the application of a power source and the development of appropriate materials and tools. For the agricultural age, it was, initially, animal power (oxen, horses) and tools like the plough. For the industrial age, it was, initially, steam power (later oil and electricity) and steel, making possible the development of machine-driven extractive and manufacturing processes. For the information age, it is the interrelated technologies of microelectronics, computing, and telecommunications.

IT is having a profound effect on personal lifestyles, on the way in which work is carried out in offices and factories, on

128

education and on health care ... on all aspects of society and the economy. A broad spectrum of previously separate areas of business – computing, electronics, telecommunications, broadcasting, business/office equipment, the media (newspapers, television, video, cable, satellite, etc.) – is converging into one 'IT industry'.[2]

Information technology is thus a necessary consideration for managers in all organizations because of this pervasive impact on external environments (social, educational, economic, etc.) and also because of the potential impact of IT on internal organizational structures and processes. Four interrelated trends have been identified as significant to the management perspective:[3]

- Multiple IT: information which would previously have been generated, stored and transmitted on paper might now be created and conveyed using a wide range of technologies: mainframe, mini, and micro-computers and distributed computing networks; a variety of data communication networks (internal and external); videotex; facsimile transmission; word processing; electronic mail.
- Dispersing IT: the trend away from a centralized 'data processing function and towards distributed, local and personal information processing using, for example, desk-top workstations linked to local and wide area networks.
- Accelerating IT: the swift pace of technological change and the rapid emergence of new technological options.
- Pervasive IT: the spread of IT into all areas of life so that people come into organizations (as staff or as customers) with some understanding of IT and expectations regarding IT support.

Key management questions are raised by these four trends. How can a coherent IT development strategy be produced and implemented, given the wide range of technologies and the rapid pace of development? How can organizational structures and technological systems be brought into line, given, on the one hand, the need for (some) centralized management control and, on the other, the trend to decentralize computer networking? How can the knowledge and expectations of new generations of IT-literate staff be incorporated and supported in organizations where

129

resource constraints limit progress in IT applications? How can technological change be accommodated without dislocation and disruption within the organization?

The successful harnessing of IT to organizational goals requires much more than technical 'know how'. IT raises strategic questions about organizational structure, management style, the nature of products and services offered, and the internal processes by which those products/services are being created and delivered. It raises a number of important 'human' considerations relating to attitudes, behaviours, and the implications for staff and customers in the ways the technology might be used. It raises significant operational issues if a decision is taken to install, say, an automated circulation system, a computer-based cooperative cataloguing process, or an online search service. Technology is a catalyst for change. But organizations evolve more slowly than do technologies, and the pace of change within an organization needs to be judged with care. Because technology has a fundamental impact on the way in which an organization works, IT developments need rigorous and careful thought on the strategic, tactical and operational levels.

For libraries, information technology is a crucial consideration. Not only does it pervade the external environments which condition staff and customer expectations. Not only can it change the nature of staff activity and customer behaviour. Not only does it have important implications for operational and management processes. Its central concern – information, or knowledge – is the raw material of library work. Definitions of IT tend to apply microelectronics-based technologies to the activities – acquisition, processing, storage and dissemination of information – which form the essence of library service.

Impact on library service
Information technology can have a major impact on four areas which, taken together, make up library service:

- raw material
- operational processes
- management processes
- customer interaction.

Traditionally, the *raw material* of library service is the library's stock – a collection of physical artefacts, usually in the form of print-on-paper (books, journals, other documents) but also including other media (sound recordings, photographs, videos, etc.). Traditional library systems are geared to the identification and retrieval of these artefacts – a particular book title, journal issue, video recording, etc. But IT can convert all these types of information-carrying artefacts into digital data for the purposes of storage (e.g. optical disc), processing (e.g. computing), and transmission (e.g. data communication networks). The traditional focus on an artefact, its format and its location – on library holdings, collection development, and bibliographic records – is replaced by a focus on information *content* and electronic *access*.

The *operational processes* of libraries involve a vast number of routine transactions (e.g. as books are issued, returned, reserved, become overdue, etc.) ideally suited to automation. Circulation control systems, cataloguing processes, systems for the ordering and acquisition of stock and for serials control can all be automated – increasingly through one 'integrated' computer system – in order to improve efficiency and productivity. Records are no longer duplicated and staff are saved much of the clerical drudgery needed to maintain manual paper-based library systems.

The *management processes* of planning and control can be considerably enhanced by IT. An integrated system can provide important stock management information. A distributed network of terminals (e.g. for the circulation system or library catalogue) can provide an opportunity for communication by electronic mail. There is considerable scope – as yet largely unrealized – for the application of computerized management information systems and decision-support systems to libraries. In addition, basic business-application software packages (word processing, spreadsheets, etc.) can be used in the library office, as in any other type of organization.

Information technology can change the nature of *customer interaction* in three ways:

- by speeding up routine processes at the library counter;
- by widening the choice of available information sources and services;
- by making library service more accessible.

131

Automated processes save time for the customer at the counter by dealing more efficiently with issues, reservations, etc.

Rather than relying on the library's own holdings, the customer can have access to remote stores of information using online or videotex networks. Rather than the old card catalogue or card index of local information, the customer can use an OPAC (online public access catalogue) or PET (public enquiry terminal) with swifter and more sophisticated searching of the information database. Facsimile transmission can speed the process of document delivery from remote sources. Computerization can aid the provision of current awareness and SDI (selective dissemination of information) services. Database management software linked to either desk-top publishing equipment or a data communication network can enable the library to 'repackage' and disseminate information in ways which give it added value – the library becomes an electronic publisher.

In addition to this enhanced range of information sources and services, IT can also widen the customer's choice in terms of points and methods of access to the library. Indeed for some disabled people, technology gives them the opportunity to use a service which would otherwise be inaccessible – 'it means the difference between exclusion and participation, limited and full functioning, failure and success'.[4] Instead of having to physically visit the building or room, the customer – using electronic networking – can have the option of 'dial-up' access to the library, 24 hours a day, from home or workplace. Libraries in some commercial concerns and educational establishments are already linked into an organization-wide electronic network giving anyone who works in the organization desk-top access to library catalogues, databases, online search services, etc. There has also been some experimentation with electronic access to public library services using public data networks – perhaps the best known being the work at Pike's Peak, Colorado.[5]

Given this exciting range of opportunities, there is a danger of librarians becoming technology-led, either because they are keenly interested in technology for its own sake, or because they feel they *should* be 'into IT' in order to keep up with the profession's trendsetters and status seekers.

For a library manager, or any manager, the key concept when considering IT is *appropriateness* – is the particular application of IT under consideration appropriate to that specific library service? For example, a small one-person library in a school or volunteer organization might not be able to justify an automated circulation control system, given the relatively small number of transactions handled at the library counter. However, that same library might be able to justify installing a microcomputer and data communications link in order to provide access to important information held either internally (using database management software) or externally (using online search services). The productivity gains would not be great enough to justify the automated circulation control system, but the service enhancement might justify the investment in a micro and a data link.

There are four reasons why library managers might invest in IT:

- Technology development and experimentation for its own sake.
- To keep up with trends and status symbols in the profession.
- To improve productivity.
- To enhance service.

The first might be justifiable in special circumstances – if the library has a particular mission (and funding) to support research. The second is not justifiable in organizational terms. The third and fourth reasons are those on which management should focus. Investment in IT can be justified in terms of efficiency (productivity) or effectiveness (service enhancement).

There are four main areas in which IT has had an impact:

- cataloguing.
- 'housekeeping' functions (circulation control, serials control, acquisitions).
- 'customer related' services (which means, in the main, access to online search services).
- interlending and document delivery.

The study[6] of IT applications in UK libraries, published by the European Commission in 1987, provides a realistic overview of the extent of that impact on large library systems (public libraries and libraries in higher education) although it does not include the large number of small libraries in schools and colleges, commerce and industry, and the voluntary sector. Of the libraries surveyed, many are using some form of computerized catalogue production (mainly still COMfiche) and some are moving to OPAC and towards networked access to library catalogues. Some academic libraries, for example, are using JANet – the Joint Academic Network – to access each others' catalogues. A number (although by no means as many in the UK as in the USA) are using resource-sharing networks such as OCLC and BLCMP for derived cataloguing. Most are using some form of automated circulation control system and some are moving towards integrated systems incorporating acquisitions and serials control. Surveys in the USA produce similar findings. Major public and academic libraries have automated their cataloguing, interlending, circulation, and acquisition functions.[7]

Thus the primary initial stimulus to IT applications in large libraries is the productivity gain that comes from automating transactional routines and cooperating with other libraries – through a third-party organization like OCLC – in the production of catalogue records.

When it comes to services which are more directly customer-related, the European Commission study gives (as a 'conservative' estimate) the calculation that 13 per cent of UK libraries offer access to online searching; with end-user searching described as 'negligible' because of the pressure imposed by time-based charges to use the service in an efficient, skilled way. The use of online is increasing rapidly in some libraries and it may be that, in this area, the study is somewhat dated. According to a survey published by the ALA in 1987, over 34 per cent of US public libraries serving populations greater than 25,000 offer database searching; and over 80 per cent of US universities provide online search services.[8] However, there is not a great deal of evidence – yet – of high-powered data communications networks, or of end-users gaining direct access to information sources without using the librarian as intermediary.[9]

The study indicates that interlending and document delivery amounts to some four million transactions a year in the UK, including demand from overseas. IT is used, in a small percentage of cases, as a means of requesting documents, and there is some – the study describes it as 'extremely low' – electronic delivery of documents using facsimile transmission. But in the vast majority of cases, interlending and document supply still involves conventional modes of requesting and delivering conventional (paper-based) documents.

The electronic delivery of electronically stored documents – that is, the concept of electronic text transfer which lies at the heart of the hypothetical 'online' or 'electronic' library – remains at the stage of research and prototype experiment, rather than viable product or system development. The 'online library' concept is based on three projected trends:

- away from providing physical documents and towards providing access to information content.
- away from buildings and locations, and towards access and networks.
- towards the convergence and integration of previously separate functions (authoring, publishing, production, dissemination) in the 'knowledge chain'.

From the customer perspective, the concept is of a single, seamless process from keying in search terms to browsing through primary text, all in one transparent and 'user-friendly' sequence conducted by the end-user at that individual's personal workstation.

It is possible to extrapolate from current technologies and build exciting, theoretic constructs of this type based on end-user access, electronic networks, dynamic information content, and radical redefinitions of fundamental concepts in librarianship like 'document' and 'bibliographic control'. The difficulty lies in applying any sort of real-world timescale to such constructs.

Electronic text transfer and the 'online' library are very much in the realms of futurologist speculation for all but a few libraries. Eventually, information technology may lead librarianship into a world 'beyond bibliography',[10] but, for the moment, the dominant library landscape will remain that of printed documents, collection development and bibliographic systems.

The current 'state of the art' of IT applications in libraries is still focussed primarily on productivity gain, although some libraries are entering a second phase of development in which the focus is on service enhancement. Within realistic planning horizons (say, the next five years), most library managers will be making investment decisions about IT on the basis of the following three arguments:

- more efficient library administration (by automating transactional routines or joining a cataloguing cooperative).
- more effective ways to deliver existing services (for example, by transferring library-generated files – such as local community or business information – onto a database or viewdata system).
- service enhancement by adding a new dimension, such as access to databases online or through CD-ROM.

Some few library managers will be concerned with a more fundamental transformation of the service – either entirely or in part – towards the 'online library' model. But this is likely to occur only in those organizations which are entrepreneurial, resource-rich, involved in the IT industry, or for which IT is a central part of the corporate development strategy.[11]

Planning for information technology

Planning for IT involves all three levels of management: senior (concerned with strategy and long-term planning); middle (concerned with the interface between strategic and operational planning); junior (concerned with the day-to-day realities of implementing operational plans). Earlier (Chapter 2), the example of automating a library's circulation control system was used to illustrate these levels: senior management taking the strategic decision to automate and setting the overall timescale; middle managers converting these strategic objectives into operational plans for implementation in their particular areas of responsibility; and junior managers putting these operational plans into effect – for example, ensuring that stock is bar-coded and staff trained.

Information technology raises a number of strategic and operational considerations. Strategic issues include:

- the potential of newly emerging information technologies.
- the impact of IT on organizational structure.
- the impact of IT on library purpose and the nature of library service.
- the cost, value and funding of IT-based library services.

This section considers, briefly, each of these in turn.

Technology changes so rapidly that it is difficult for management to make informed investment decisions. In the last decade, for example, in the UK

- the video industry presented consumers first with a choice of proprietary standards (Philips V2000, Sony Betamax, JVC VHS) and then with an industry 'shake-out' which has left VHS as the dominant standard – and left many consumers with equipment which is no longer supported by new products.
- the home computer industry followed a similar pattern with early market leaders (such as Sinclair) now effectively defunct.
- the online search industry has evolved from dumb terminals dedicated to specific hosts to micro + datalink access to a choice of hosts; from slow to fast speeds of data transmission; from online formulation of queries to search strategies developed offline and conducted by computer; from host print-out to local downloading.
- computer aided catalogue creation has evolved from COMfiche to OPAC.
- library 'housekeeping' systems have evolved from relatively crude (batch processed) circulation control systems to sophisticated (real-time) 'integrated' systems offered by a confusing array of vendors.
- teletext has become established as a useful medium for up-to-date information at 'headline news' level.
- public viewdata (Prestel) stumbled badly but has begun to recover ground with a mix of carefully managed databases and interactive services; private viewdata has emerged as a powerful tool, in certain contexts, for information dissemination and interactive communication.
- business-standard microcomputers have evolved to a level where they have as much processing power as the mini-computers of a decade ago; the 'front end' of such computers has become increasingly 'user friendly' with the use of WIMPs (windows, icons, the mouse, pointers) rather than a learnt command language.
- computer systems have evolved from terminals hard-wired to a mainframe or mini-computer to distributed processing networks of powerful microcomputers.

- digital telecommunications have emerged with the development of national and international public data networks and private leased lines.
- optical disc technology has emerged as an important new dimension to IT with: audio CD already well established in the home entertainment market; CD-ROM causing a considerable stir as a medium for archive storage and sophisticated offline information retrieval; and a number of ambitious multimedia packages (such as the 'Domesday' or 'Emperor I' projects) beginning to appear.

Such a list (not intended to be exhaustive, but merely indicative) shows: how much technological change of relevance to library service there has been in the last decade; how much time and energy needs to be invested in order to keep up with technological developments; how much money it is possible to spend in this area, and how easy it is not to get value for that money (by buying a system which is soon to be superseded or which does not fulfil its promised potential); and how difficult IT investment decisions can be.

Technology has the potential to effect fundamental change on the organizational structure of a library. Libraries, traditionally, are relatively self-sufficient organizations. For example, a traditional university library would support its carefully developed collection of stock holdings with a full range of technical systems (for bibliographic work, stock processing, binding and conservation, etc.) and reader services (subject specialist assistance, etc.), all encompassed within the library organization. On the other hand, IT can place the library in a 'web' of electronic connections with: other libraries; information sources and services; suppliers and other specialist agencies; library customers. Already, much technical service work is contracted out: stock processing and binding/conservation to specialist agencies, and bibliographic work to library suppliers or bibliographic utilities. Through IT, the focus for reader services is less on holdings and more on electronic access to a network of remote resources (information sources, document delivery systems, specialist research services). The 'online library' model suggests that, in some cases, customer access to the library will be through an electronic network rather than a personal visit.

There is a clear structural difference between the centralized 'self-sufficient' library and the 'networking' library based on decentralization, cooperation, and the contracting-out or buying-in of services. These 'networking' characteristics have positive advantages:

- more efficient resource deployment (through cooperation, leading to rationalization);
- more effective customer service (providing access to a wider range of resources);
- improved responsiveness to change (offering greater flexibility of structure).

However, the traditional library structure based on a relatively self-sufficient collection and in-house support services has important values in relation to the behavioural characteristics of customers who enjoy browsing and the delights of serendipity. In addition, cooperative systems can sometimes grow in size and complexity to the point at which the cost of supporting a large and complex infrastructure outweighs the benefits to the individual member-library. The point is made strongly, in the USA, by Thomas Ballard[12] who mounts a powerful attack on the prevailing orthodoxy of resource-sharing, network technology, interlending, and access to distant sources. Ballard's viewpoint is supported, from a different perspective, by Charles Hildreth in a report[13] on *Library automation in North America* undertaken at the request of the European Commission as a companion to the 12 studies of EC member states. Hildreth suggests that the role and function of the large, centralized utilities are challenged by a move to decentralized systems and local networks.

An important strategic issue for library managers on both sides of the Atlantic, is to find a structural balance between self-sufficiency and networking, having regard to economic constraints, technological possibilities, and customer behaviours and preferences. The nature of this balance will depend, to an extent, on the purpose of an individual library and its priorities for service provision. IT highlights the information-providing role of libraries. It tends to assume a customer who is adult and interested in a specific subject area or a particular document. This focus is reflected in the move to redesignate many libraries and library-related agencies in order explicitly to include *information services* as well as *library* in the organization's title.

However, many libraries have objectives other than those which are related to the information function. Educational objectives, objectives related to recreation and leisure, social objectives are all an important part of library work. Unless the primary objectives of the service are kept clearly in focus, IT may have a distorting influence on planning, resource allocation, and service development.

Thus IT challenges library managers in the areas of organizational structure and service priorities. It also challenges the traditional model of library service – not just the way that libraries do things, but also the fundamental perceptions of cost, role, and value.

IT-based systems and services are expensive to set up and run. If the result is service enhancement – offering something 'extra' which customers perceive as being additional to the 'basic' service – might not those high costs be passed on, justifiably, in the form of a direct charge payed by those customers who choose to use this enhanced service? Otherwise, these high costs are borne, indirectly, by all of the library's customers many of whom do not need or use such a specialized service.

Thus IT highlights the crucial debate about the funding of library service: should the whole customer community pay indirectly so that the service is made freely available as a community resource to be used by those individuals who choose to do so; or should those people who choose to use the service pay for it through direct charges; or should the funding of libraries involve a mix of both methods? In this IT challenges the traditional concept of a 'free' library service – the traditional perception that library activities and forms of information delivery should be free or low-cost to the individual customer.

By becoming linked to concepts of commercial enterprise and 'added value' services, IT has become a catalyst for polarity within the library and information services profession. Consider the following list of contrasts:

information access	library holdings
direct charging	'free' service
commercial development	public investment
'added value'	'comprehensive and efficient'
market demand	social equity

There is a conflict here. On the one hand are those who wish to develop the business opportunities presented by information resources, using IT to provide 'added value' services, that is services for which a charge can be made because the customer perceives them as being of greater value than the 'basic' level of library provision. This additional value is created because the service is:

- specialist: tailored specifically to an individual customer's need and in more depth than the generalist service usually offered.
- timely: speedier than usual services.
- repackaged: information gathered and synthesized for the customer, rather as an information scientist might do in a specialized library.
- tangible: producing a tangible end-product (online search print-out, state-of-the-art report, etc.) which the customer keeps.

On the other hand are those who stand for equality of opportunity and 'comprehensive' service provision, who perceive a danger that high-tech added-value services will create a 'two-tier' library, accentuating the division between information-rich and the disadvantaged information-poor.

There is, obviously, the danger of conflict between public interest and commercial enterprise – just as there is the opportunity for positive partnership between public and private sectors to widen customer choice by applying technological developments to information resources. This debate is taking place on both sides of the Atlantic and there is a need to find a sensible synthesis which brings together the valuable elements from both sides of this apparent divide. The precise nature of that synthesis is not clear – and will vary from library to library – but what is clear is that strategic thinking of a high order is necessary in order to resolve the ambiguities regarding library structure, purpose, and charging policy which are accentuated by developments in information technology.

Once the strategic decisions have been taken, operational issues become crucially important. Many of these concern careful planning of the installation and 'running in' process, and are well covered elsewhere in the literature.[14] Running through strategic, tactical, and operational levels, however, is the human dimension – the response of customers and library staff to technology.

Behavioural considerations

Information technology which enhances service will require changes in behaviour from both staff and customers. IT which is installed for productivity gain may not have much direct impact on customer behaviour – but it will have a major impact on the nature of the work done by library staff. Behavioural considerations are thus a crucial part of the effective management of IT.

Customers need to be kept informed of IT developments partly out of general interest and courtesy, but also so that they understand why new behaviour patterns are required. To take a simple and obvious example, an automated circulation system usually requires customers to produce a bar-coded borrower card. Remembering to carry this card will be a significant change in behaviour for customers in those libraries where borrowing a book previously meant simply filling out a form at the issue counter.

Developments considered by library management to be 'service enhancements' may not always be seen that way by some customers. Replacing a card catalogue with COMfiche can reduce the number of simultaneous access points (unless a significant number of terminals are installed), and replace a familar retrieval system with a fiddly process of lighting, alignment and focussing. Replacing cards or COMfiche with an OPAC means that the customer has to become accustomed to a computer keyboard. However 'user friendly' the on-screen prompts may be, there will always be some customers who take time and find difficulty in adjusting to keystroke access. Customers may need not just information, but active guidance and support in using the new system.

Similarly, putting a community information file onto a database or viewdata system may well enhance the service – but may also inhibit the potential customer. The data may be more current and the indexing more sophisticated than in the former card file – but many of the people for whom the service is designed may not be computer-literate and may feel hesitant about attempting to access the system. Again, active staff support and 'user education' will be necessary if customers are to gain full benefit

142

from the enhanced service. It is important that these issues of information, user education and staff support are thought through when planning the installation of an IT-based service.

As well as possible inhibitions about using IT, a second aspect of customer behaviour has to be taken into account. Most IT service enhancements require the customer to either use a terminal (OPAC, videotex, CD-ROM, etc.) or consult a member of staff (for example, to arrange or formulate an online search). But in many libraries (particularly public and some academic libraries), customers operate on a 'self-service' basis. In the main, they go directly to the shelves and browse. This raises three questions:

- How can the library ensure – if resources are constrained and are being directed into computer systems, electronic networks, and access to remote sources – that the on-site collection of stock remains large and vital enough to support fruitful browsing?
- How can computerized information systems replicate the browsing process?
- How can 'self-service' customers be encouraged to modify their behaviour and explore the electronic information services now provided by the library?

The first question is a matter for strategic planning, financial management, and cost-benefit analysis. The second is one to be addressed by system vendors and electronic publishers (who claim that it *is* being addressed by the development of more sophisticated file structures and search software). The third question reinforces the need to keep customers informed of IT developments, incorporate considerations of marketing and promotion into the planning process for new services, and ensure that library staff can provide appropriate guidance and customer support.

Two other points regarding customer behaviour need to be considered. One is that the introduction of an IT-based service in one area of the library may increase pressure of use in another area. For example, the introduction of online access to bibliographic databases is likely to produce an increase in interlending traffic as customers using the online service identify a greater range of references and so request more documents.

143

The second point follows from this – the possibility of system overload (for the library) and information overload (for the customer). The online search or computerized SDI service may be used in a somewhat indiscriminate way, simply because it is available. The result may be that customers become aware of a large number of documents which could prove to be of marginal importance, but which they feel they *should* examine. This increases pressure on the customer (to wade through all the identified documentation) and on the library (to satisfy all the requests for online searches, SDI services, and interlibrary loans). In this situation, direct charging can act as a regulator, inhibiting indiscriminate and 'casual' use and ensuring that online searches and SDI services are both precisely formulated and of real value to the customer.

In order to provide the guidance and support needed by some customers, library staff have to feel comfortable with IT. The importance of the human dimension in management has already been stressed, and IT provides an illustration of the need for good interpersonal relations, open communications, a comprehensive and supportive programme of training, and a management style which encourages staff to feel involved in decision-making and developments within the organization.

IT investment to achieve productivity gain implies a saving in the staff budget (although it may well mean an increase in other areas of expenditure). That saving can be presented in a positive manner: staff will no longer endure the time-consuming drudgery of clerical routines; they need spend less time 'behind the counter' and 'in the backroom', and will have more time for direct customer service. However, some staff may see automation in a different and negative light:

- possible redundancy: in many industries, productivity gains from automation have come from a reduction in the size of the workforce. Automation may be seen as a threat to job security.
- possible redeployment: 'backroom' staff may not enjoy the prospect of working directly with customers. Technical services people do not necessarily make good reader services people.
- a threat to status: years of accumulated experience and wisdom in the 'old ways' will count for nothing. Status will now be

conferred on the technocratic 'whizz kids'.

- deskilling: some of the skill, pride and interest in the job will be lost. Cataloguers, for example, may feel that the 'professional' content of their job is lessened if the library derives most of its bibliographic records from a national agency (like the British Library or Library of Congress) or a cataloguing cooperative (like OCLC).
- health and safety fears: anxiety about the possibly damaging effects of exposure to computer screens.
- technofear: inhibitions or actual fear of using unfamiliar technology.
- technofervour: over-enthusiasm for new technology which can have two negative effects – it alienates other members of staff, making them feel more negative about the new installation, and it leads to expectations of the new system or service which are unrealistically high, and bound to be disappointed.

Open and honest communication can help alleviate and overcome these negative viewpoints. Management should take care

- not to leave matters to rumour and speculation.
- not to issue bland statements that 'It won't make any difference' (if it won't, why spend all that money!).
- not to raise expectations too high regarding the wondrous capabilities of the new system or service.

Throughout the process of decision-making and subsequent planning for installation, staff should be kept informed and involved – for example, by producing regular 'IT bulletins' on strategies and progress, or by arranging for staff who will be using the new system to visit comparable installations elsewhere. A full programme of training should be arranged so that staff feel confident and supported in their new tasks – and time should be allowed for staff to familiarize themselves with the new equipment by 'playing' with it after installation. Individual counselling can also play an important role as staff work through the implications of technological change for their jobs and future careers.

Introducing any form of IT – be it a full-scale integrated

system to replace manual 'housekeeping' routines or a micro-computer for access to online databases — is a case study in the importance of:

- open communications;
- participative management;
- support for staff through training and development .

Just as IT reinforces the importance of staff 'feeling good' about themselves and their work, so it also underlines two key issues of management style and structure. The first is the trend towards networking, partnerships, and collaboration rather than self-sufficiency. The use of IT requires that libraries liaise — and sometimes work closely — with IT system and service vendors whether these be:

- library systems suppliers (ALS, Geac, CLSI, etc.)
- bibliographic utilities and cooperatives (OCLC, BLCMP, etc.)
- database publishers and online hosts (Pergamon, Dialog, Datastar, etc.)

This highlights the point made earlier (Chapter 4) that managers spend much of their time dealing with people who work for other organizations and not with 'their own' people. Libraries and library suppliers work in partnership in a mutually dependent and beneficial relationship — and the management style employed needs to reflect this.

Arising from this is the need — in order to fully exploit IT — to build into the library's management team some IT expertise. The effective management of three fundamental resources — staff, finance, and technology — requires expertise additional to the skills of librarianship. The library manager must develop this expertise personally or bring people with this expertise into the library's management team or collaborate with specialist sections elsewhere in the parent organization.

The second issue accentuated by IT is the tension which can exist within an organization between the forces for centralization and those for decentralization. For example:

- an automated order/acquisition system can centralize and

standardize the process of stock selection. An individual branch or departmental library may be unable to exercise the autonomy, for example, of choosing to buy stock directly from a non-mainstream supplier.

- an automated circulation system can monitor and record the relationship between items overdue and fines received, highlighting discrepancies and so working against the tradition of local discretion in applying the regulations regarding fines.
- an automated and shared cataloguing system will require certain standards when a catalogue record is originated which may be different (often, more comprehensive) than the level of record needed by the library originating the entry.

Thus automated systems can be resented because they inhibit local-level autonomy and flexibility. IT may lead to greater efficiency and effectiveness, but it also brings its own bureaucracy – procedures which have to be followed because 'the system' requires them.

Financial implications
Investment in IT requires decisions based on cost/benefit or risk/return analysis. Potential benefits (in terms of productivity gain, service enhancement, or financial return) are assessed, costs and risks are considered, and the decision is taken.

The costs that need to be considered are of three types:

- *Capital* costs (i.e. once-and-for-all expenditure on plant and equipment): these include hardware and software, and also any peripherals that may be needed. A major system installation may, for example, involve considerable expenditure on furniture, cabling, antistatic carpeting, air conditioning, a 'clean' power supply, etc.
- *Revenue* costs (i.e. expenditure which will continue or recur): this includes the cost of maintenance and also an amount set aside to cover depreciation and system development. It also includes the running costs – for example, the costs incurred during online searching.
- *Staffing* costs: setting up a system involves staff (training; bar-coding stock; retrospective catalogue conversion, etc.) as does the continuing operation of IT systems and services. Additional

147

staff may be needed, or existing staff may receive an increase in salary to reflect new IT-related tasks and responsibilities.

As well as identifiable *costs*, there are a number of *risks* which will also need to be assessed:

- Both IT and the IT industry are evolving rapidly, with technologies, products and vendors in a state of constant change. Products are 'hyped' and commercial suppliers often have only a short track record. In such a volatile climate there is the risk of choosing a product which does not match up to expectations or a supplier who fails to deliver the level of service which has been promised. A carefully documented specification of what is required, supported by some form of legal contract, is a necessary safeguard.
- If an automated library system is installed, the library becomes 'locked in' to that particular system vendor and therefore subject to the charges made by that vendor for the operation, maintenance and development of the system. These costs are becoming a substantial budget item for many libraries. As Ian Lovecy writes:[15] 'Undoubtedly there is a danger of systems development squeezing both staffing and stock budget into non-existence.'
- If an IT-based service is installed, there will be a measure of uncertainty and guesswork regarding the likely take-up of the new facility. Two types of 'risk' result from this. With some services – such as online searching – customer usage will mean library expenditure, and there is risk involved in deciding how much money to set aside for this. Some services will be installed on a self-financing basis, particularly at a time when resources for new services are severely constrained. There is risk involved in projecting usage and setting charges at a level judged likely to provide an adequate income.

Making a direct charge for use of certain IT-based services has number of outcomes (in addition to the fundamental point that charging may inhibit use and work to the disadvantage of some potential customers). It provides a financial return on investment which can help sustain and develop the service. It can help regulate use at a manageable level. It can enhance perceptions and expectations of the library by providing customers with 'added value' services. But it has two important implications for library managers.

The first is that it involves management in decisions about pricing. Traditionally, library charges are modest and marginal. In contrast, online search costs are often quite substantial. Customers are not used to paying 'real money' for library services, nor, in the main, are they likely to perceive information as a costly commodity. Use of new and unfamiliar services is likely to be extremely price-sensitive, and careful market research will be needed to ensure that prices are pitched at the 'right' level.

The second is that it involves management in quality control. Charging for a service empowers customers; it gives them the right to require and demand a certain standard of service. It thus focusses attention on the need to identify measures which can be used to indicate the quality of library performance.

Successful retailing requires:

- careful marketing
- sensitive pricing
- rigorous quality control

If library managers are to 'retail' services to customers, then they too must pay attention to these issues.

IT and management control
Questions of quality control and performance measurement lead to the concept of strategic information systems planning (SISP). This is the process of developing a systematic information strategy within an organization to support that organization's objectives. It has two key elements

- Determining information needs in relation to organizational objectives and the requirements of individual managers.
- Devising and implementing information systems to meet those needs.

This process of analysing 'information management' requirements may not lead to a computerized solution, but the emergence of SISP has been linked directly to developments in IT because of the ability of computer-based technologies to capture, process and transmit data. Computer systems have the capacity not just to gather, analyse and present useful management information; they can also be used for 'modelling' – building hypothetical models and scenarios which can be applied to test decisions by showing likely outcomes.

Librarians need good management information and support for decision-making. Many large libraries already use computer systems to handle transactional routines and those systems generate a substantial amount of potentially useful data. These automated systems could provide an element of management information for those libraries. For example, the development programme for the 'electronic library' concept in Pike's Peak, Colorado, incorporates support for management decision-making as well as automation and integration of administrative routines.[16] The vision is of a system which the library manager can interrogate in order to keep a regular on-screen check on how well the library is performing.

However, as yet, automated library systems have concentrated mainly on processing transaction data, not on producing management information. As Peter Brophy concludes:[17] 'The majority of management information produced from automated systems is relatively crude, highly structured and very much a system byproduct.' The structured data sets produced by such systems do not help senior managers with strategic decision-making, nor does the present generation of systems have any 'modelling' capability to enable library managers to test alternative options. However, vendors are beginning to incorporate 'report writers' into the system software. These enable library managers to specify the data sets to be analysed, the nature of the processing to be carried out, and the format of the final report. This marks a step away from fixed data sets prescribed by the system to more flexible analysis determined by the library manager. It is possible that the next generation of library systems will migrate towards SISP, creating a third possible justification for investment in IT: productivity gain; service enhancement; and also improved support for management decision-making and control.

Conclusion
Information technology can be used as an illustration to highlight

almost all of the key themes which emerge in this book:

- The rapidity, pervasiveness, and inevitability of change, in both external environments and internal processes.
- The importance of leadership thinking and strategic planning to resolve: issues of library purpose (so that IT is applied appropriately); issues of structure (libraries, like computers, can be networked or stand alone); issues of value and funding (concepts of 'added value', implications of charging, the need to balance the interests of customers and providers in the exploitation, through technology, of information resources).
- The importance of careful tactical and operational planning to manage change and ensure the successful implementation of IT systems and services.
- The importance of the human dimension in management, and the need to support staff – through good interpersonal relations, open communications, training and development opportunities, a participative and 'sharing' management style – at a time of change.
- The importance of putting the customer first: having regard for customer behaviour, and providing guidance and support as needed.
- The importance of marketing, quality control, and performance measurement.
- The recognition that management in a time of change involves *risk* management. In the IT context, library managers take risks on: investment decisions; possible obsolescence; possible increasing system costs; pricing, if customers are to be charged for a service; the level of return in terms of take-up and value as perceived by the customer.
- Recognition of the need for a strong framework of financial control. The implementation of IT requires careful costing and can involve 'profit and loss' accounting by which income is set against expenditure.
- The importance of management information, and the potential of IT in the development of management information systems.

If any operation is to work efficiently and effectively, then planning, organization and people (the subjects covered in Chapters 2, 3 and 4) need to be properly managed. Technological

151

change is a catalyst which – along with economic and political change – is stimulating library management to look beyond these basics and pay attention to:

- quality and value of service.
- enterprise and accountability in financial matters.

The next two chapters focus on issues of quality control (Chapter 6) and financial management (Chapter 7).

References

1   The classic research studies on the 'post-industrial' society are American. See, for example:
    Daniel Bell, *The coming of post-industrial society; a venture in social forecasting*, New York, Basic Books, 1973.
    Marc Uri Porat, *The information economy; definition and measurement*, Washington DC, US Department of Commerce, Office of Telecommunications, 1977.
    Forest Woody Horton and Donald Marchand (eds.), *Information management in public administration*, Arlington, Information Resources Press, 1982.
    A useful British text is: Tom Stonier, *The wealth of information: a profile of the post-industrial economy*, Thames Methuen, 1983.
2   See, for example, the 'map' of the information business published by the American Society for Information Science; *Journal of the American Society for Information Science*, 35, (3), May 1984, pp.170 – 8.
3   See Michael Earl, 'Emerging trends in managing new information technologies' in *The management implications of new information technology*, ed. Nigel Piercy, Croom Helm, 1984.
4   Barbara Baskin and Karen Harris (eds.), *The mainstreamed library*, p.87.
5   Kenneth E. Dowlin, *The electronic library; the promise and the process*, New York, Neal-Schuman, 1984.
6   The European Commission has published reports on *The state of the art of the application of new information technologies in libraries and their impact on library functions* for each of the 12 member states (publication EUR 11036, Commission of the European Communities, Directorate-General for Telecommunications, Information Industries and Innovation, Luxembourg, 1987).
7   See Mary Jo Lynch, *Libraries in an information society: a statistical summary*, Chicago, ALA, June 1987.

8   *Ibid.*

9   *The use of information technology by information services; the Aslib information technology survey 1987*, Aslib, 1987. The survey shows end-user searching in only 11% of responding libraries, and only 15% of respondents using a data network operating at more than 1200/1200 bps.

10 Frederick Kilgour, *Beyond bibliography*, the third British Library annual research lecture (1984), BL, 1985. Kilgour provides one of the most ambitious expressions of the 'online library' concept in describing EIDOS (Electronic Information Delivery Online System) and his vision of its impact on the behaviour of information users.

11 Some of the material in this section is based on research commissioned by OCLC (Europe) and a paper delivered to the 1988 annual conference of the UK Library Association's Information Technology Group (Bob McKee, 'Systems astigmatism' in *It's news*, September 1988). I am grateful to OCLC and to LAITG for permission to recycle the material here.

12 Thomas H. Ballard, *The failure of resource sharing in public libraries and alternative strategies for service*, Chicago, ALA, 1986.

13 Charles Hildreth, *Library automation in North America: a reassessment of the impact of new technologies on networking*, (EUR 11092), Munich, K. G. Saur, 1987.

14 See, for example, Ian Lovecy, *Automating library procedures: a survivor's handbook*, LA, 1984. Also the series of 'Case studies in library automation' published by the (UK) Library Association.

15 Lovecy, *Automating library procedures*, pp.124 – 5.

16 Noted in Peter Brophy, *Management information and decision support systems in libraries*, Gower, 1986, pp.109 – 10.

17 *Ibid.*, p.128.

6 Quality and value: the 'control' function

Introduction

The 'management cycle' is a continuous process of planning, implementation, and control. Clearly, control is necessary to check that matters are 'going according to plan' – to monitor and evaluate progress, anticipate potential problems, and receive feedback which can then be built into the planning process.

In part, the 'control' process takes place informally. The astute and well-organized manager will keep an eye on things through casual conversation and observation; this is an important dimension in the technique of 'managing by wandering about'. The various meetings which make up the planned communications structure of an organization also contribute to the control process. One important function of such meetings is to review progress and performance.

But in most organizations, there will also be a formal control process based on some form of management information system (MIS). This is a planned system for gathering, processing and disseminating information so that effective management decisions can be made. It enables a manager to ask three types of question:

- how is the organization doing?
- what situations need to be looked into?
- which course of action is better?

The third question involves a sophisticated process of 'modelling' by which a manager can test various hypotheses and alternatives. The first and second questions involve analysis of data relating to the performance of the organization – measuring actual performance against pre-set standards or targets, and analysing any deviation. The heart of such a system, then, is:

- information – a set of data – relating to organizational performance;
- and a mechanism by which that information is collected, analysed, and disseminated.

The excellent documentation on planning and control produced in America by the Public Library Association (with specifics related to public libraries, but principles which are generally applicable) describes the basic steps towards MIS in exactly these terms:[1]

1. Determine exactly what information is needed, with attention to how each item of information will be used within the library.
2. Develop a co-ordinated system of data collection, clearly assigning the responsibility for each measure, including how it is to be collected, how often, and by whom, to ensure that all the needed information is collected once and once only.
3. Design a way to analyze and disseminate the information that has been collected to every unit that needs it.

A fourth point might be added: ensure that staff responsible for collecting data understand why it is being collected and recognize the usefulness and relevance of the exercise. If staff feel involved in the process they will take more care to produce accurate and timely statistics.

There is considerable interest in this process of management control – and particularly in the question of what measures should be used to indicate performance – in library management at present. In both the USA and the UK, there is extensive literature on the subject[2] and there have been, in recent years, a number of important initiatives in this area. Of particular importance is the manual of *Output measures for public libraries* prepared for the Public Library Development Program in the USA.[3] What is significant is that the 12 measures identified in the first edition (1982) remain unchanged in the second edition (1987), suggesting that – in public libraries at least – some consensus is beginning to emerge regarding these output indicators.

There are two reasons for this current focus. One is accountability at a time of constrained resources and the pressure to demonstrate 'value for money'. The other is a concern for quality and customer satisfaction, linked to the consumer movement and a 'customer first' approach to service. The latter is reflected, in the UK, by the work of the National Consumer Council[4] and by bodies like the Local Government Training Board whose approach to providing better service to customers is summarized in *Getting closer to the public.*[5] The former is reflected in the work of the Audit Commission (set up to audit the 'economy, efficiency and effectiveness' of UK local authorities) and in the pressure from government to apply 'performance indicators' to all areas of public service – health care, education, social services, etc.[6] Richard Luce, UK Minister for Arts and Libraries, puts the government position clearly:[7]

> When library authorities are equipped to set meaningful objectives, cost the resources they put into the related services and measure their success, they will be in a much better position not only to obtain good value for money but to demonstrate to the public and to Parliament that they are doing so.

'Performance', then, can be viewed from three perspectives:

- That of the resource-provider, concerned with *value* (what good does it do? what benefits are achieved?) in relation to costs.
- That of the service-provider, concerned with *quality* (how good is it?) as well as value. In this context, *quality* means capability – the library has the capacity (in terms of its resources) to achieve a certain level of service.
- That of the customer who will interpret *quality* of service in terms of a more or less satisfying experience when visiting the library, and *value* in terms of the benefits gained from that visit.[8]

Some of these elements can be quantified and measured. If quality means capability then it can be measured in terms of the resource inputs to the service. Traditionally, this was the way in which the quality of library service was measured – by comparing actual provision with the recommended levels of resourcing given in a set of 'standards'. If these resource inputs are related to outputs (that is, the work performed; number of books issued, enquiries dealt with, interlending requests processed, etc.) then it should be possible to calculate costs and gain some indication of efficiency.

However, effectiveness – the impact and outcomes of the service – is much less easy to measure. Value (in terms of benefits gained) and quality (as reflected in customer satisfaction) cannot be quantified by a process of data collection and analysis. Something more than a databased management information system is needed.

What to measure?
In discussing control systems with the top management of successful companies, Goldsmith and Clutterbuck identified four recurrent themes:[9]

- tight controls on finance.
- constant feedback on results.
- close attention to business planning.
- setting high standards and expecting people to stick to them.

The importance of planning has already been emphasized, as has the need to develop and reinforce an organizational 'culture' which supports high standards of customer service. Finance is the subject of the next chapter. In this chapter, the focus is on 'feedback on results'.

Libraries, like many organizations, have the potential to collect large amounts of data – particularly those libraries which have installed automated systems. However, data alone does not indicate 'results' and a large amount of data can be counter-productive; in the effort to wade through it, significant figures might be overlooked. The first principle of an effective control system is *simplicity* – the system is easy to administer and focusses on a few, clearly defined and understood, measures. The second principle is *relevance*, or, as Goldsmith and Clutterbuck put it, *astuteness*. This means that the system must be useful for decision-making; and also that it provides an appropriate and balanced profile of the organization's activities.

Performance indicators influence behaviour, and an ill-considered set of indicators can misdirect energies or pay attention to one area of the organization's work at the expense of other areas. To take a classic indicator often used in library management, the number of loan transactions may indicate the levels of busy-ness at the issue desk; but it provides no information on other equally important areas of the library's stock use (for example, in-library use for study or reference purposes). If this indicator, alone, is given primary attention by management, then library performance will be measured by the number of issue transactions; and there will be a tendency for the decisions of service point managers (on stock selection, staff deployment, service promotion, etc.) to be influenced by this fact. The number of issues may rise – but at the expense of other areas of service provision.

If the system is simple and relevant, then it is also likely to meet other basic criteria: cost-effective; accurate; timely; and acceptable to all those concerned with it. This last point is particularly important. Control systems can be resented, because they create work (the bureaucratic form-filling that is often involved in data collection) or bring pressure (to achieve 'results'), or because they imply a lack of trust. If service point managers and front line staff resent the controls, there will be attempts to 'beat the system' or 'fiddle the returns' – both of which will be damaging to a system the effectiveness of which depends on accurate and timely information.

What types of library data, then, can be collected as the basis from which a few key performance indicators can be derived? Most libraries maintain statistics on a variety of *inputs* and *outputs*, for example:

- inputs
  - finance; income and expenditure by source and use.
  - staff; number employed in various categories.
  - stock; holdings, additions, etc. in different locations and formats.
  - service points; number, size, opening hours, etc.
- outputs
  - customers; number of registered users.
  - circulation; number of loan transactions.
  - interlending; number of requests.
  - reference work; number of enquiries.
  - other programmes and services; e.g., number of storytelling sessions for children, visits to housebound and institutionalized people, user-education sessions, etc.

In the UK, the *Public library statistics* published by the Chartered Institute of Public Finance and Accountancy (CIPFA) provides a good example of this approach.[10] Each year figures are produced (first, 'estimates' for the financial year, and subsequently 'actuals' for that year) which give a detailed breakdown of: income and expenditure; staff; service points; stock; interlending; issue transactions; request services; and so on.

However, data without comparison is meaningless. The CIPFA figures provide raw material for analysis, and also include a number of derived statistics which enable comparisons to be made between local authorities of differing population sizes. These include:

- ratio of library staff to population.
- bookstock per 1,000 population.
- annual book issues per head of population.
- requests per 1,000 population.
- expenditure (under a range of headings) per 1,000 population.
- income (under a range of headings) per 1,000 population.

Comparisons between different library services must be considered with caution, because of differing local circumstances and policies. However, it is possible to subdivide public or academic libraries into 'groups' or 'families' for the purpose of comparison. The Institute of Public Finance has produced a classification which clusters UK public libraries into groups,[11] and SCONUL (the Standing Conference of National and University Libraries) groups UK universities using an interesting mix of location, size and heritage.[12]

Comparison of one library with others in its 'family', using figures such as those produced by CIPFA and SCONUL, can provide some useful pointers. For example, CIPFA figures might indicate that a particular public library service has:

- no service point open for 45 or more hours per week.
- a lower than average number of staff for the size of population.
- a low total bookstock for the size of population; a much smaller percentage of reference books than seems usual.
- a low number of requests for the size of population; a relatively poor performance in supplying requested books.
- comparatively high expenditure on premises, computer costs and debt charges.

- a relatively high income from the hire of materials, but no income from specific grants.

By itself, this analysis does not mean much. But it provides a useful checklist to trigger management attention, and subsequent action to investigate these deviations.

However, in any comparison between library services, it is important to take into account local conditions, service priorities, and the political context which largely determines policies and resources. This is important in all types of libraries, not only those which are part of local government service. The importance of the political dimension is stressed, for example, by John Allred in discussing the evaluation of academic library services.[13]

Essentially, three types of comparison are possible in order to give meaning to basic statistical data:

- ratios; comparisons which, for example, relate inputs to outputs
- time series; comparison of a set of statistics over time to identify trends
- standards; statistics of actual performance are compared with some form of set standard. This could be a set of nationally recommended standards, the average performance attained by a group of comparable libraries, or objectives set by the individual library in the form of service targets or budget estimates.

A useful example of this last type of comparison is provided in the CIPFA statistics by the figures given for request services. These give the percentage of requested books supplied within 30 days and 60 days. Within Metropolitan Boroughs, the average performance is to supply 61% of requested books within 30 days and 81% within 60 days. The spread of performance is between 43% and 78% supplied within 30 days and 71% – 94% supplied within 60 days. This is a particularly interesting indicator because it relates directly to customer service, and poor relative performance will be a trigger for management investigation.

Good examples of the use of ratios and time series are provided by the statistics for UK polytechnic libraries produced by COPOL (the Council of Polytechnic Librarians) and published as an appendix to the *Report by the Minister for the Arts on Library and Information Matters during 1987*. These are reproduced, with the COPOL commentary, at the end of this chapter.

The commentary gives an excellent example of the way in which ratios and time series can be used to indicate trends in the changing relationship between inputs and outputs. These COPOL figures give a revealing statistical profile of the resource position in polytechnic libraries. The (unstated) implication may well be that increasing pressure on resources is leading to a reduction in the quality of service. However, the figures do not show this. They provide useful 'resourcing indicators' but they do not, in themselves, provide 'performance indicators' relating to the quality and value of library service.

COPOL and CIPFA figures may indicate how much money was spent on books, what percentage of the total library expenditure that comprised, how many books were bought, the average cost of a book; and how these inputs have changed over time. They may indicate how many books were borrowed, and how this indicator of output has changed over time. But they do not indicate how valuable these books were found to be, or the quality of interaction between customer and staff at the enquiry or issue desk.

In commercial enterprise, the 'bottom line' is the profit margin and the return (in financial terms) on investments made. Libraries are, usually, non-profit organizations and there is no similarly tangible and quantifiable 'return' on investment.

One response to this is to argue that use is the only true indicator of performance. If a customer receives a service of acceptable quality and value, he or she will return to use the service again. If the service proved not to be acceptable or appropriate, it will not be used again. Levels of use compared over a time period can give some indication (by implication) of the quality and value of a service to its customer community. So figures for the number of people in 'live' membership (i.e. actively using the library), the number of issues, reference enquiries, book requests, etc. provide some indication of service quality if it is accepted that there is a correlation between volume of use and customer perceptions of quality and value.

Analysis of these figures in relation to the overall size of the customer community (percentage of the population in 'live' library

161

membership; number of issues etc. per head of population) may give some indication of market penetration. But it is important to relate these output figures to wider considerations. For example, the COPOL figures show a 17% drop in the number of issues per customer (line 19) over three years. In that period the number of issues actually went up by 12.7% – but the customer population increased by 44.4%.

Return on investment can be expressed in terms of overall levels of use and market penetration. It can also be expressed – by relating inputs to outputs – in terms of efficiency. The Audit Commission has suggested 'issues per staff hour' as a possible efficiency measure and this has been used, for example, by Surrey in a comprehensive performance review of library service in each geographic area of the county.[14] However, such measures need to be approached with caution. When reviewing library service in Cleveland (the English county, not the American city), the Audit Commission found no correlation between number of staff on duty and number of books issued. In his commentary on the Commission's review, Frank Regan, the County Librarian, pointed out that the staff-to-issue ratio is affected by a wide range of factors to do with priorities for service provision and the nature of the building itself. Rather than being, of itself, an indicator of greater or lesser relative efficiency, the staff-to-issue ratio is a figure to trigger management investigation in order to discover or confirm why there is deviation over time or between service points within the same library system.

Efficiency is not the same thing as effectiveness and, indeed, a service which becomes more efficient (i.e. gets more work out of a given set of resources; gets more output from the same input) may, in the process, become less effective. The COPOL figures show an increase of 40.3% in the number of customers served per member of library staff. This apparently massive increase in efficiency (caused essentially by a large increase in custom with no comparative increase in resourcing) may well lead to a poorer quality of library service; with staff under strain and unable to give adequate time and attention to each individual customer.

This discussion of various types of library data and their analysis emphasizes four points:

● Statistics are interrelated. One figure, taken in isolation, can give a partial and misleading impression. It is important that statistics be analysed as a 'set' in order to get the full picture.

● It is sometimes difficult to determine what a particular set of statistics actually indicates. An apparently significant statistical deviation is not, in itself, a 'performance indicator'. All that it indicates is the need for management to investigate and explain that deviation.

● Performance must be set into the political context of policy and priorities. One library may have a large volume of use (measured in issues per head of population) which is handled with great efficiency (measured as issues per member of staff). Another may have a lower 'score' on both counts – fewer issues per head of population or member of staff. But if that other library has policies which give priority to other aspects of service (reference work, user education, outreach, etc.), then the 'lower score' simply reflects a differing set of policies and priorities. In any evaluation of library service, the starting point has to be the objectives of that service.

● The return on investment in library service is expressed in the quality and value of that service as experienced by its customers. This is not susceptible to quantitative measurement and 'hard' data analysis. It is a 'soft' field involving analysis of expectations, perceptions and experiences.

This last point is emphasized in the work on performance measurement carried out, in the USA, by the Public Library Association:[15]

> Three kinds of information contribute to the evaluation of the library's current performance: the statistics that most libraries keep routinely; responses on the citizen, user, staff, and student surveys; and measures of the library's achievements relative to specific objectives or services, that is, performance measures.

As the PLA document points out, these three sources of information complement and overlap one another to give a multi-dimensional picture of the library. What is significant is the emphasis that is given – in addition to a carefully constructed set of statistics – to 'soft' methodologies using observation and survey techniques.

Observation can provide indications about: the number of

people using the library; the average length of time spent in the library; in-library use of facilities and materials (including stock used but not issued); and staff availability (i.e. the amount of time customers have to wait for service).

Surveys of the whole potential customer community can indicate: general perceptions and attitudes regarding the library; awareness of library services; levels of market penetration; and reasons for non-use of the library. Surveys of library customers can reveal: who uses the library, how often, and for what; satisfaction with the service, for example, in terms of attractiveness, accessibility, availability of materials, etc. Surveys of particular customer groups can provide more detailed information regarding a specific market sector to which the library service may wish to give priority. Surveys of staff are also important. As the PLA points out:[16] 'Staff members are usually well aware of the strengths, weaknesses, and problems of the library in the delivery of services. Their attitudes have substantial impact on the implementation of any library policy. Finally, their experience in dealing with the public provides insight into user needs and patterns of use.' This mix of 'hard' data and 'soft' feedback is reflected in the manual of *Output measures for public libraries* produced by the PLA. Of the 12 measures identified, 3 are concerned with 'fill rate' (that is, the percentage of customers who had their hopes – for example, of finding a particular title – fulfilled). This information can only be collected by means of a regular 'materials availability' survey.[17]

The move towards 'soft' feedback from surveys to complement 'hard' data analysis is reflected, in the UK, in the work of bodies like the National Consumer Council and the Local Government Training Board. Both *Measuring up* (NCC) and *Getting closer to the customer* (LGTB) emphasize the importance of customer feedback, and a number of local authorities in the UK have employed market research companies to carry out surveys of public opinion regarding local government services. The conclusion of the National Consumer Council in *Measuring up* is that a qualitative evaluation (based on checklists, questionnaires, interviews, discussions, etc.) set within a broad statistical context seems the most promising way of investigating a service's achievement. This is also the approach taken by King Research in developing a manual of performance indicators for UK public libraries; the research takes an holistic approach, drawing connections between input resources available, outputs achieved, and user satisfaction with the service.[18]

Thus, 'control' of the quality and value of library performance involves a range of elements:

- statistical analysis;
- customer feedback;
- staff feedback.

Consideration of these elements must be related to the library's stated aims and objectives. Achievements can only be defined in terms of intentions. This – and the mix of hard and soft methodologies involved – suggests that, in the context of library service, it is misleading to talk of performance *measures*. Assessing the benefit a customer or community gains from its library service is, in the final analysis, a matter of informed value-judgement rather than measurement.[19]

Methodologies and mechanisms
Mechanisms for data collection and methods of statistical analysis clearly have a part to play in the 'control' function of library management. Rather than relating local data to nationally recommended standards of resource provision, the current focus is on relating data on actual performance to locally determined objectives and targets. In the UK, the Library and Information Services Council has stated its view that there is 'no prospect of any return to quantitative standards' for public library service and its belief:[20] 'that library services should be judged in relation to their local circumstances, the policies and achievements of similar authorities, professional opinion and generally accepted management criteria, rather than in relation to a uniform standard.'

Similar thinking lies behind the work on planning and control carried out in the USA by the Public Library Association as part of the Public Library Development Program. The 'Foreword' to *A planning process for public libraries* notes that the publication marks 'a major change of direction' for the PLA – from the provision of national standards, to the development of a planning process to be applied by individual library systems:[21] 'Through the planning process outlined here, libraries will set up standards appropriate to the local conditions and needs; design strategies to reach them; and inaugurate a planning cycle which involves continuous monitoring of progress and regular adjustment of objectives as community conditions and needs change.'

This switch of approach reflects the need for control mechanisms appropriate for a time of change. National standards may work in a context of uniformity and stability. However, in a context of diversity, with changing customer needs and resource frameworks, a pattern of locally determined objectives and regular planning cycles seems more relevant.

Statistical analysis is supported by a number of other mechanisms and methodologies. The process of data collection and transmission requires a reporting mechanism and the management information system (MIS) for most libraries involves various regular data returns on a daily, weekly, monthly, quarterly or annual frequency. These are sometimes supplemented by a written report. Most line managers will be expected to produce an annual report which supplements data with written commentary on important matters. A useful addition to a library's MIS is an annual report form which poses key questions to which line managers are asked to respond.

This move towards data complemented by dialogue is reflected in the handbook on *Performance review in local government* produced by the Audit Commission. This gives a series of 'review questions' for each local government service (including public libraries) designed to guide the discussion between auditor and local authority and to set statistical indicators into the context of local policy and professional judgement.

Discussion with and between staff is an important part of the control process. Margaret Slater's research indicates that customers perceive libraries as a duality – services and staff – with staff a vital element in determining the level of customer satisfaction. Equally, front line staff should have a keen perception of quality and value because they work at the 'sharp end' of customer interaction and service provision. Library performance depends not just on the efficiency and effectiveness of systems, but also on the quality of service given by staff. Development discussions organized as part of a staff appraisal system provide an opportunity to review service quality. In addition, it may be possible for line managers to institute 'quality control' (QC) circles in individual service points and departments. QC circles are small groups of staff, working together at local level, who meet regularly to discuss issues of quality. This has a number of advantages:

- focussing attention on 'quality' as a topic for consideration and action.
- bringing the consideration of quality down to local, 'grass roots' level.
- giving members of staff involved in QC circles a sense of participation in considerations of quality. If an individual feels 'ownership' of a particular issue (that is, feels a personal involvement in the issue) then he or she is more likely to give it careful and continuous consideration.

Just as the control system overlaps with the process of staff development, so it also overlaps with stock management. As Roger Stoakley, County Librarian of Somerset, has written:[22]

The stock of the library system is the core around which the whole service is built. It is the second largest item in the budget after the cost of staffing. The selection of stock, its maintenance and encouragement of its use constitute the fundamental skills of the librarian. If we fail in these essentials then the total service will be a failure.

Stock management is a subject which requires a book of its own in order to do it justice.[23] However, in terms of the library's overall control system, two aspects can be highlighted:

- efficiency: analysis of the performance of suppliers (time taken to deliver ordered items, quality and extent of bibliographic and processing services, support for the selection process such as the provision of lists of published items and approval collections, the range of titles exposed, the unit cost of servicing agreements, etc.) in order to ensure optimum cost benefit.
- effectiveness: analysis of stock movements (using the data derived from automated systems) to develop policies to optimize stock availability through collection development, loan procedures, and a balance between on-site holdings and access to items through interlending networks.

Stock management is one area where systems automation (for example, of ordering and acquisitions, and of circulation control) has given library managers the opportunity to derive useful management information from transactional data. This will be an important area for development in the next generation of integrated library systems.

In addition to these in-house mechanisms for the collection and analysis of data and staff perceptions, there is also a need to collect feedback from the library's customer community. Feedback from customers involves similarly 'soft' methodologies to those used with library staff: surveys using questionnaires, interviews, group discussions, public meetings, etc. Many service organizations – for example, hotels and restaurants – provide forms on which customers are invited to comment on their experience of the organization in general or on particular aspects of service. This is a simple demonstration of the 'customer first' approach which could easily be applied in libraries. *Measuring up* provides a 'user success questionnaire' which asks customers six simple questions about the purpose of their visit to the library and their satisfaction with the service.[24]

However, there are a number of difficulties with 'soft' survey methods. Because satisfaction levels are determined by preconceptions and expectations, and responses are sometimes influenced by a desire to give the 'right' answer, surveys can produce results which are more subjective than objective. The library 'image' (see Chapter 2) can have a bearing on survey responses. *Measuring up* recognizes that the questions about 'satisfaction' in the user success questionnaire are too generalized; that customers should instead be asked if they have found what they were seeking in the library. This provides a more precise and objective response. Relevant here are the questions about 'fill rate' developed in America. The manual of *Output measures for public libraries*[25] suggests four such output measures:

- reference completion rate – percentage of reference enquiries which are completed.
- title fill rate – percentage of specific titles sought which are found.
- subject and author fill rate – percentage of specific subjects and authors sought which are found.

- browsers' fill rate – percentage of browsers finding something to their liking.

The use of experienced survey personnel and a carefully predetermined checklist of points for discussion can help to increase the value and objectivity of customer feedback. Two good examples are given in *Measuring up*. One is the 'quality wheel' giving a framework of general consumer criteria for service evaluation. The other is a checklist devised to prompt consumer groups in their evaluation of library service. Both are reproduced at the end of this chapter.

There is, of course, the possibility that customers will interpret the opportunity to comment as an invitation to criticize. Good service will be accepted without comment and the feedback will focus on relatively trivial 'niggles'. Again, structured interviews and guided discussions will help to give a more balanced assessment of customer viewpoints.

In addition to reports, discussions and surveys, there are also techniques of observation, and of inspection or testing. A well-known and somewhat controversial example is the 'unobtrusive testing' of reference services, by which those carrying out the test act in the manner of ordinary enquirers and then record the quality of answers given.

One final mechanism needs to be added – customer complaints. If a customer has taken the trouble to complain formally about an aspect of the service – however trivial, petty or wrong-headed that complaint may appear to be – it is important that the complaint receives a prompt and courteous response. Complaints are, in fact, a form of unsolicited feedback from individual customers. As such, they can make a positive contribution towards service improvement.

This range of methods and mechanisms suggests that it is inappropriate to focus simply on performance *measures* or even on performance *indicators*. The mix of 'hard' data and 'soft' methodologies suggests a continuing process of performance *review*:

- reviewing the data on resource inputs and service outputs – using key ratios, time series, 'family' comparisons, and comparison with set objectives and targets – in order to trigger management attention and investigation.

169

- reviewing feedback from staff: through the regular process of reports, meetings, and appraisal/development interviews; using 'quality circles' or meetings at local, service-point level at which the agenda focusses on issues of quality; and by means of questionnaires and surveys.
- reviewing feedback from the customer community (both users and non-users) produced by a range of methods: observation, questionnaires, surveys, discussions, etc.

This process of review is much more than the implementation of a management information system (although a simple and relevant MIS can be an important contributor to the process). Because it involves all staff – in data collection and analysis; in providing individual and collective feedback; in generating feedback from the customer community – the review process gives continuous attention to service quality at all levels of the organization. Considerations of quality and value become part of the library's 'culture', and not just a concern voiced occasionally by senior management.

References

1 Vernon E. Palmour *et al.*, *A planning process for public libraries*, pp.84 – 5.
2 Prominent in the literature is F. W. Lancaster whose *The measurement and evaluation of library services* (Washington DC, Information Resources Press, 1977) is now complemented by *If you want to evaluate your library* . . . (Graduate School of Library and Information Science, University of Illinois, 1988).
3 Nancy A. Van House *et al.*, *Output measures for public libraries: a manual of standardized procedures*, 2nd edition, Chicago, ALA, 1987. This is a revised edition of Douglas Zweizig, *Output measures* . . . , Chicago, ALA, 1982.
4 *Measuring up: consumer assessment of local authority services: a guideline study*, National Consumer Council, 1986. The subject of *Paper 3* in this set of six studies is the public library service.
5 *Getting closer to the public*, Local Government Training Board, 1987.
6 Audit Commission, *Performance review in local government: a handbook for auditors and local authorities*, HMSO, 1986. The handbook consists of ten sections, including one on *Leisure and libraries.*
7 *Report by the Minister for the Arts on Library and Information Matters during*

1987 (HC 332), HMSO, March 1988, para.16.

8 The distinction between 'quality' (i.e. capability) and 'value' (i.e. benefit) is made by R. M. Orr, 'Measuring the goodness of library service: a general framework for considering quantitative measures' in *Journal of documentation,* **29**, (3), September 1973, pp.318 – 32.

9 Goldsmith and Clutterbuck, *The winning streak,* pp.49 – 50.

10 Chartered Institute of Public Finance and Accountancy, *Public library statistics.* CIPFA publishes annual volumes of *Estimates* and *Actuals.*

11 Phillip Ramsdale and Stuart Capon, *Costing systems in public libraries: report of survey,* Institute of Public Finance occasional paper no. 3/87, IPF, 1987.

12 Taken from the SCONUL data given in Appendix C to *Report by the Minister for . . . 1987.*

13 John Allred, 'The evaluation of academic library services' in *Management issues in academic libraries,* ed. Tim Lomas, Rossendale, 1986.

14 Graham Combe (ed.), *Performance review in the library service: the Surrey experience,* Public Libraries Research Group, 1987.

15 Palmour *et al., A planning process for public libraries,* p.48.

16 *Ibid.,* p.138.

17 Nancy A. Van House *et al., Output measures for public libraries,* p.52f.

18 *Manual of performance indicators for public libraries,* study funded by the Minister for Arts and Libraries, administered by the British Library Research and Development Department, and carried out during 1987 and 1988 by King Research Ltd. At the time of writing (January 1989), a draft manual is due to be released for discussion.

19 This point is made in Sue Stone, *Library surveys,* 2nd revised edition, Bingley, 1982.

20 'Library and information services in 1987: review by the Library and Information Services Council', paras. 12 and 13. Published in *Report by the Minister for . . . 1987.*

21 Palmour *et al., A planning process for public libraries,* p.xi.

22 Roger Stoakley, *Presenting the library service,* Bingley, 1982, p.64.

23 See, for example, Tony Houghton, *Bookstock management in public libraries,* Bingley, 1985.

24 *Measuring up: paper 3, public libraries,* pp.3, 21 – 3, 25.

25 Nancy A. Van House, *Output measures for public libraries: a manual of standardized procedures,* 2nd edition, Chicago, ALA, 1987.

Appendix D to *Report by the Minister for the Arts on Library and Information Matters during 1987* (HC 332), HMSO, 1988.

Appendix D

Polytechnic library statistics 1983-84 to 1985-86

Preface 1. The following statistics are taken from annual reports on *Statistics of Polytechnic Libraries* compiled by COPOL (the Council of Polytechnic Librarians). Statistics have been gathered since 1979 – 80, but the present table gives only the three most recent years as definitions and categories changed between 1982 – 83 and 1983 – 84, rendering some comparisons very difficult. All figures given are mean averages which enable trends to be compiled which make allowance for variations in response each year and for variations between polytechnics in response to request for certain items of information. As numbers of polytechnics supplying certain data vary in some items, all comparisons have been calculated from raw data using matched pairs.

Commentary 2. The figures for the three years show a number of ups and downs. Over the three years, the library spend has increased more than the polytechnic spend, but showed a serious decline in 1985 – 86 compared with 1984 – 85.

3. Line 8 shows a great increase in the numbers of people served by the libraries. These include both full-time and part-time staff and students (with research and postgraduate students increasing over the period by over half). These much larger numbers of people to be served account for a considerable decline

in the library spend per person served and in bookstock per body, with an increase of 40% in the ratio of people served to library staff. The spend on salaries has increased roughly in line with inflation but the spend on salaries as a percentage of total library spend declined in 1985 – 86.

4.   Over the three years, expenditure on books went up by 12.0%, which is far behind the LISU[1] price index increase of 17.5%. Expenditure on periodicals, for 6.3% fewer periodicals received, went up by 10.5% but the Blackwell periodicals price index published in the Library Association Record (LAR) each year increased by 30%. Such increases put a great strain on the library staff and stock. Total issues over the three years went up by 12.7%, though the great increase in people served gave a decline in issues per person.

5.   The overall picture thus shows polytechnic libraries facing difficult problems of greatly increased numbers of users, greatly increased prices of books and, especially, periodicals with budgets which have not increased in line with these two factors.

---

[1]Library and Information Statistics Unit, Loughborough University.

Item	1983–84	1984–85	% Change on 1983–84	1985–86	% Change on 1984–85	% Change over 3 years
1. Total polytechnic spend (£000)	18,268	17,553	− 3.9	19,131	+ 9.0	+ 4.8
2. Total library spend (£)	825,223	871,290	+ 5.6	886,798	+ 1.8	+ 7.4
3. *Library as % of poly spend*	*4.52*	*4.73*	*+ 4.6*	*4.58*	*− 3.2*	*+ 1.3*
4. Total people served	8,960	11,931	+ 33.2	12,938	+ 8.4	+ 44.4
5. Library spend per person (£)	88.12	77.58	− 12.0	71.44	− 7.9	− 18.9
6. Library spend on salaries (£)	447,440	464,977	+ 3.9	489,393	+ 5.3	+ 9.4
7. *Salaries as % of library spend*	*55.3*	*56.8*	*+ 2.7*	*55.4*	*− 2.5*	*+ 0.18*
8. People served per library staff	160.9	209.4	+ 30.1	225.7	+ 7.8	+ 40.3
9. Spend on books & pamphlets (£)	133,013	129,168	− 2.9	148,964	+ 15.3	+ 12.0
10. *Books & pamphlets as % of library spend*	*17.6*	*15.8*	*− 10.2*	*17.1*	*+ 8.3*	*− 2.8*
11. Books & pamphlets spend per person (£)	15.26	12.33	*− 19.2*	12.86	+ 4.3	− 15.7
12. Books added to stock (units)	13,775	12,858	− 6.7	13,153	+ 2.3	− 4.5
13. Total bookstock	280,561	286,249	+ 2.0	284,477	− 0.6	+ 1.4
14. Bookstock per person	31.7	25.4	− 19.9	24.8	− 2.4	− 21.8
15. Periodicals (titles) received	2,349	2,248	− 4.3	2,201	− 2.1	− 6.3
16. Spend on periodicals (£)	121,192	130,349	+ 7.6	133,879	+ 2.7	+ 10.5
17. *Periodicals as % of library spend*	*14.8*	*15.2*	*+ 2.7*	*15.2*	*0.0*	*+ 2.7*
18. Total library issues	255,138	260,773	+ 2.2	287,492	+ 10.2	+ 12.7
19. Issues per person	28.9	23.0	− 20.4	24.0	+ 4.3	− 17.0
20. ILL, borrowed	5,923	5,621	− 5.1	5,637	+ 0.3	− 4.8
21. ILL, loaned	866	987	*+ 14.0*	890	− 9.8	+ 2.8
22. On-line searches	213	255	*+ 19.7*	287	+ 12.5	+ 34.7
23. LISU average book price (£)	17.49	18.46	*5.5*	20.55	*11.3*	+ 17.5
24. LAR periodicals price index (£)	84.73	100.81	*19.0*	110.18	*9.3*	− 30.0

Notes on items as enumerated in the table

1. Data as given by Polytechnic Finance Officers Group (PFOG).

2. Excludes capital expenditure on automation or equipment but includes any non-recurrent expenditure on material

3. Because of different bases for calculations it is not wise to compare this proportion with that for university librari

4. 'People' includes all staff and students served by libraries, whether full-time or part-time. Because of high deman made on polytechnic libraries by part-time students they are equated for this calculation with full-time students. Note al that in the three years covered the average numbers of postgraduate students have risen from 337, to 435 and to 511, increase overall of 51.6%.

9. 'Spend' includes both recurrent and non-recurrent expenditure.

15. 'Received' includes gifts and exchanges.

20 & 21. ILL = Inter-library loans. The figures show movement from borrowing to lending.

22. On-line searches are normally restricted to staff and postgraduate researchers. These increases therefore reflect increase in research activity in polytechnics.

'Consumer criteria for service evaluation' from *Measuring up: paper 3, public libraries*, National Consumer Council, 1986, p.v.

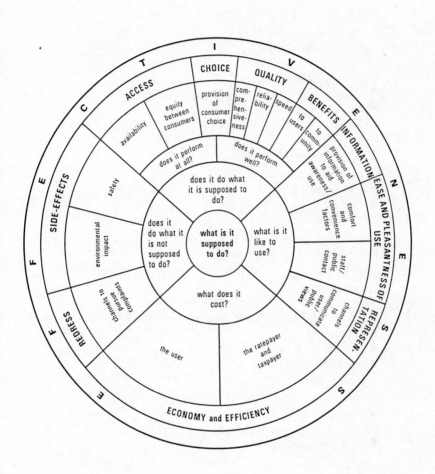

'The consumer checklist', *ibid.*, pp.3. 28.

The aspects of service covered by the checklist were as follows:

- convenience and location in relation to:
  - shopping facilities
  - public transport
  - car parking
  - prams/pushchairs
- external information and signposting
- convenience of opening hours for:
  - adults
  - children
- entrance to buildings
- interior lighting
- layout of bookstock/internal signposting etc.
- facilities for special needs
  - old/disabled
  - large print books
- service/facilities for children
  - efforts to encourage children
  - stock
- meetings/lecture room facilities
- staff (whether helpful and knowledgeable)
- seating
- catalogue/index systems
- range of books
  - fiction
  - non-fiction
- availability of books
- ease of renewals
- records and tapes.

7 Enterprise and accountability: financial management in a context of constraint

Introduction

Finance underpins all organizational activities. It enables staff to be employed, technology to be applied, buildings to be erected, equipment to be bought, services to be provided. If an organization cannot acquire adequate finance, or does not use its finance efficiently and effectively, it will fail to meet its objectives. Financial management is thus an integral part of each element in the 'management cycle' of planning, implementing, and control. In order to be implemented, policies and objectives have to be translated into plans or programmes for action. Central to that planning process is an assessment of the resources that will be needed in order to accomplish the plan, and a calculation of the cost of those resources. By calculating costs and setting these against the benefits which are expected as the outcome of the plan, and then placing this cost-benefit analysis in the wider context of the organization's objectives and overall financial position, it becomes possible to rank plans and programmes into priority order, to set financial timescales for major projects, and to allocate resources accordingly.

As plans are implemented, financial considerations become a crucial part of the 'control' function of management. Estimations will have been made regarding income that the organization is likely to receive and expenditure that will be incurred. Management needs to keep a close watch on the relationship between actual income and expenditure and the previously estimated levels of income and expenditure on which plans, programmes and timescales will have been based. On a day-to-day basis, this is usually done through the budgeting process. Each department within the organization has a budget which sets limits on expenditure and it is the responsibility of departmental management to see that expenditure is kept within those limits. Similarly, each department may have targets for income, and performance will be monitored in relation to those targets.

As well as the continuous process of control through budget management, organizations and departments will also, from time to time, be subject to audit, by which the financial control system and other associated aspects of management performance are scrutinized. Auditors may be internal or external to the organization and may either limit themselves to comment on the organization's accounting processes and financial management, or may be given a wider remit to conduct a 'management audit' which explores all aspects of management performance. In the UK, for example, the role of the Audit Commission is to ensure that local authorities and public bodies comply with law and good practice in their financial control, and also to see that they show 'economy, efficiency and effectiveness' in the use of resources to deliver services.

Control is also exercised through an organization's accountability to its owners or to those responsible for its governance. A commercial organization will produce an annual report containing various audited financial statements (such as a profit and loss account for the year under review, and a balance sheet which sets assets against liabilities). This will be presented at an annual general meeting of – in the case of a publicly quoted company – the shareholders. In the commercial world, these figures provide the ultimate control mechanism. Their analysis will determine the level of confidence in the company's prospects and that level of confidence will determine the company's share price and ability to raise money in the various financial markets.

A similar process, although without the regulating mechanisms of the money markets, applies to organizations which are not in the commercial sector. An annual report, containing statements of income and expenditure, will be presented at some form of annual general meeting. Confidence in the organization's management and prospects will be determined, largely, by analysing these figures in relation to the 'estimates' for that year or the corresponding figures for previous years.

Strong financial planning and control, then, is vital to an organization's future prospects, and a critical factor in determining the level of confidence which those with a 'stake' in the

178

organization (as part of its ownership or governance) have in its management. This is particularly so at a time when economic constraints are increasing the pressure on management to account for the ways in which resources are used and to seek out new ways by which income might be generated. In many organizations – most noticeably in the non-commercial public sector – traditional approaches to financial management are changing to reflect this need to demonstrate accountability and 'entrepreneurialism' or enterprise.

The financial context

The process of financial analysis, planning, and control operates on three levels:

- the external environments of legislation, audit, the economy, and the money markets; issues of company law, taxation, etc.; strategies for investment and raising finance.
- the organization's assets and liabilities: management of current and fixed assets, and of short-term and long-term liabilities; matters such as the capital 'gearing' – that is, the ratio of debt (funds raised by borrowing) to equity (funds raised through shareholding) – of a company.
- budget management (using planned limits on expenditure and targets for income) at departmental level.

The library manager is involved, primarily, with the third – departmental – level of financial management. The library is unlikely to be, of itself, a corporate entity; it is more likely to be a department within a larger organization. Matters to do with external financial environments or the overall management of assets and liabilities are likely to be the concern of a separate department specifically concerned with financial matters. Financial resources are available *to* the library, but are not actually held *in* the library (other than relatively insignificant sums of 'petty cash' or a 'float' of small change in the till). When the library spends money, it does not do so directly. The usual practice (in the UK) is to 'raise an official order' authorizing payment which is then passed to the finance department for action. Similarly when the library receives money it does so on behalf of its parent organization. It is the organization (not the library itself) which issues invoices and to which cheques are payable. Cash income (from fines and fees) is passed on, by the library, to the finance department to be administered.

This process does have potential inefficiencies and difficulties. The bureaucracy of an 'official order' is unacceptable to some potential suppliers, particularly those small 'alternative' or 'radical' bookshops which can provide important material from minority publishers. It also becomes difficult for the library to take advantage of any cash-with-order discounts. Cash management strategies are out of the library's hands: with no control over when accounts are paid, the library may not be able to benefit from the fast-payment discounts which are sometimes offered by suppliers and publishers. If all income is passed to a central administrative unit, it becomes difficult to ensure that income generated by the library service is actually credited to the library's budget.

There are some instances when the wider financial world of asset/liability management and external economic environments has a direct impact on library management; for example, when an organization has to cut back on expenditure because external economic factors have led to a shortfall in projected income. This has happened in a large number of commercial organizations on both sides of the Atlantic where financial management in a time of recession has led to cutbacks in corporate overheads – often including a significant reduction in resourcing for the company's library or information unit. Dealing with 'the cuts' has also become a commonplace of financial management in UK public sector libraries as a result of the government's policy of reducing public expenditure; and this experience may well be mirrored in the USA as government gets to grips with the Federal budget deficit.

Pressure from central government to reduce expenditure and determination by local government, in some places, to oppose this policy and maintain or improve levels of service has produced a liquidity crisis in some UK local authorities. Current assets (i.e. those which can be quickly converted into cash) are not sufficient to meet short-term liabilities (i.e. those obligations which need to be met within a relatively short period of time). A number of local authorities, faced with this situation, have decided to improve liquidity by converting fixed assets (such as buildings) into cash by a process of sale and lease-back. Some public library services have found their buildings (and indeed their book stock) converted into capital assets and 'cashed' in this way. However, on the whole, library managers tend to be concerned with the day-to-day operation of budgets and financial reporting systems rather than the strategic levels of financial management to do with assets, liabilities and the economic environment.

Thus, a commercial organization will produce a balance sheet (setting assets against liabilities) and a profit and loss account (setting income against expenditure) which will be subjected to a process of 'ratio analysis' in order to assess that organization's liquidity (ability to meet short-term obligations), asset management (ability to convert assets into income), debt management (ability to meet long-term debts), and profitability. This type of statement and analysis is not usually appropriate for a library, unless it operates as a corporate entity. The library is more likely to be a single departmental budget centre within the organization. It is also likely to be regarded as, primarily, a spending rather than income-generating department. In commercial organizations, the library is usually regarded as part of the corporate 'overhead' – that is, the costs incurred centrally in order to support the company's activities. The year-end figures for the library-as-department (in both public and private sectors) are likely to show expenditure and then income (to give a 'bottom line' figure for *net* expenditure) itemized under a number of budget headings, such as those used in the CIPFA public library statistics (expenditure on staff, bookstock, etc.; income from fines and fees, hirings, etc.).

Comparing these two types of financial statement indicates two important differences of approach. The structure and emphasis of the commercial organization's accounts focus on *profit* (income less costs equals net surplus), while a library's accounts, traditionally, focus on *expenditure* (costs less income equals net spending).

When a commercial organization's figures are itemized in detail for internal management purposes, a separate set of figures is often produced for each *product*. It is thus possible to monitor the performance of each product in terms of income generated and costs incurred. The library's figures are detailed under *budget headings* itemizing different types of income source and spending area. It is not usually possible, from the structure of these figures, to identify income generated and costs incurred by individual 'products' or services (e.g. children's services, reference services, etc.).

These distinctions reflect the traditional differences between a *business* and a *service* approach. It is important for a business to focus on profit and the financial performance of individual products: output and outcomes are expressed in financial terms. For service organizations, operating as part of the corporate overhead or supported by public funding, the focus is on efficient deployment of resources. Inputs are subject to financial control and scrutiny. Outputs and outcomes are expressed by usage data and satisfaction levels (see Chapter 6); not primarily in financial terms.

However, some elements of the 'business' approach to financial management are beginning to be applied to library service. The library manager's financial responsibility has been limited, traditionally, to the budgeting process and specifically to the control of an expenditure budget. However, this responsibility is widening as a result of the pressure for accountability and enterprise, linked to the move, in many organizations, to devolve key aspects of management to the local level of the individual service unit. Library managers are now involved in:

- income generation: the library is no longer regarded simply as an 'overhead'. In 'closed' communities (such as universities or commercial organizations) the library may 'sell' its services to other departments within the organization, or individual departments allocate resources to the library rather than the library's budget coming from a central fund. In 'open' communities like those served by the public library, the pressure is to diversify the resource base, reducing dependence on centrally allocated funds. In both cases, there is an attempt to express one aspect of performance in terms of income received.

- costing: analysing costs in detail – often at the level of unit cost (that is, the full cost, in detail, of a single process or action) – in order to apportion expenditure to specific areas of activity. It thus becomes possible to produce figures for library activities which equate to the 'cost of sale' figures produced,

182

in business, for individual products.

- performance budgeting: financial statements which express performance by setting income against costs. These become appropriate if the library is operating a service on a self-funding basis (by which income from the service pays for the costs of that service) or with the intention of generating additional net income.

In these ways, libraries – even in the public sector – are no longer seen simply as 'part of the overhead' or as a spending department granted a budget from centrally deployed resources. Rather, they become 'cost centres'. Costs (and income) are disaggregated and apportioned to individual 'cost units' – service points, functional departments (e.g. acquisitions, cataloguing, interlending), service programmes (e.g. user education programmes, events for children, public library 'outreach' programmes). It thus becomes possible to relate costs to perceived benefits in a more precise way.[1]

Public sector libraries in the UK are being encouraged by government to explore the possibilities for 'joint ventures' with private-sector businesses, and to investigate the potential for contracting out aspects of library service to competitive tender.[2] The first – if not yet the second – of these is also becoming a feature of library service planning in the USA. Both these moves accentuate the need for precise statements of unit costs and service outcomes.

The remainder of this chapter looks at the traditional library budget, and then at the issues of income generation, costing, and performance budgeting which are becoming increasingly important to the librarian-as-financial-manager faced with pressure to be enterprising, accountable, and business-like.

The library budget
To coordinate financial management across the library system, two subsystems are needed:

- a reporting/accounting system: to deal with the flow of money into (fines, fees, etc.) and out of (stock purchases, etc.) the library; and to monitor that flow.
- a budgeting system: to estimate future income and expend-

iture (planning), and to monitor actual figures so that variations from the estimates can be identified and investigated (control).

These subsystems are linked to the organizational hierarchy by the process of authorizing expenditure. The authority to spend should be clearly defined (in terms of budget areas and cash limits) and line managers given that authority should also take on responsibility for regulating their spending so that it falls within the authorized budget limits. So, for example, a branch librarian in a public library or a subject librarian in an academic library may be given authority/responsibility for a portion of the money to be spent on stock.

The budgeting cycle begins with the process of estimating expenditure under two general headings:

- 'revenue' or 'recurrent' expenditure; that is, all day-to-day operating expenses, staff salaries and other costs, spending on library stock, etc.
- 'capital' expenditure; that is, major non-recurrent items of expenditure such as the cost of building or refurbishing a library, buying a new vehicle, upgrading the computer system, etc.

There is a measure of overlap in that 'capital' expenditure may have 'revenue' implications (for example, buying a new mobile library may mean employing additional staff), or, if capital expenditure is funded by borrowing, there will be recurrent debt charges. But, in general, organizations tend to treat the revenue budget and the capital programme as two separate items for consideration and decision-making.

On a day-to-day basis, library managers are less concerned with the capital programme than with the revenue budget. Capital expenditure accounts for around 6.6% of overall expenditure in both public and university libraries in the UK.[3] The traditional library budget for revenue expenditure has four key features:

- It is 'historical' with estimates for the next year based largely on expenditure in preceding years.
- It is a 'line' budget, dividing expenditure into broad cate-

184

gories (staff, books, etc.).

- It operates on a yearly cycle, with no carry-over from one year to the next.
- It is subject to time lag, with estimates calculated a considerable period in advance of actual expenditure.

All four of these features can cause difficulties. 'Historical' budgeting – because it is based on past precedents and not future objectives – tends to reinforce the status quo and inhibit radical change. A 'line' budget makes it difficult to use anything other than a historical base for estimates, and can also limit the library manager's financial flexibility; 'virement' (that is, the authority to move funds from one budget heading to another) is usually strictly limited.

The yearly cycle imposes artificial constraints which can affect spending decisions. Any money left in the budget at the end of the accounting year will be 'clawed back' by the parent organization, rather than carried over for the library's use. There is thus pressure on the library manager to spend up to budget limits – and many library suppliers can tell stories of librarians on minor spending sprees in February and March, emptying the book fund before the close of the financial year.

The time lag between estimates and actual expenditure means that the budget is affected by inflation which, over time, reduces the real value of money. A budget may show an increase, in *cash* terms, over the previous year's figures. But if that increase is less than the rate of inflation, then the budget will have been reduced in *real* terms, that is in terms of actual spending power. In some instances inflation allowances are added to the budget (for example, to meet increased staff costs resulting from a pay award). However, inflation allowances do not always cover the real increased cost. The price of books, for example, consistently rises faster than the 'rate of inflation' (as measured in the UK by the Retail Price Index) so an inflation allowance based on RPI and added to the bookfund would mean a reduction, in real terms, of spending power to buy books. It is often the case that budgets are 'cash limited' – that is, no further additional allowances can be made and any increased costs have to be met within the existing budget limits.

There have been some attempts to move away from 'historical' and 'line' budgets to a process of budgeting based on activities and priorities. 'Zero-based' budgeting disregards historical precedent and begins with the financial equivalent of a 'blank sheet of paper' so that each area of expenditure has to be justified anew at the start of the planning and estimating process. 'Performance' budgeting is based on individual areas of activity and service, including calculating the costs of that activity. Both seem attractive in theory – linking the estimating/budgeting process more closely to the process of determining service priorities and monitoring service performance – but both are complex and time-consuming to put into practice.[4]

When library budgets are broken down into component parts, a clear pattern emerges which is common for all types of library. David Liddle offers the following indicative breakdown for 'a fairly typical public library service' in the UK:[5]

Staffing costs, salaries, wages and oncosts	56%
Building costs, heat, light, rates, repairs, painting, debt charges, central charges	23%
Library materials, books, records, newspapers, etc.	18%
Running costs, printing, stationery, furniture, etc.	3%

James Thompson and Reg Carr suggest that UK university library budgets (excluding the sort of building-related costs and central charges of David Liddle's second category of expenditure) break down roughly as follows:[6]

Staff	55%
Acquisitions	35%
Binding	4%
Sundries	6%

COPOL figures (see Chapter 6) suggest a similar division: around 55% on staff and 32% on acquisitions, divided between 17% on books and 15% on periodicals. Guy St. Clair and Joan Williamson quote a comparable breakdown, with books and other stock accounting for 20 – 30%, in relation to the one-person library.[7] Figures from the USA suggest a similar profile: in public libraries, spending on staff accounting for around 58% of the budget with acquisitions representing about 16% of spending; in academic libraries around 50% of the budget spent on staff and 30% on acquisitions.[8]

What these figures indicate is the relatively small extent of the library manager's discretion and room for financial manoeuvre. Much of the library's expenditure is fixed and controlled outside the library, for example, building costs and debt charges. In other areas, such as the staff budget, there are considerable restrictions on the library manager's freedom to act and on the speed with which changes can be made. The only substantial expenditure area over which the library manager has full and immediate control is the acquisitions budget – and a certain amount of that will be committed in advance to periodical subscriptions or standing orders for reference titles. As Liddle notes, these figures help to explain why, if a budget reduction is imposed during a financial year, the library manager has little option but to cut the book fund.

For many librarians, then, financial management will mean management of all or a portion of the acquisitions budget. This, in itself, poses interesting questions. In the public library context, should each branch be given a fixed 'slice' to spend and manage, or should the fund be retained centrally, with each branch bidding for money in the light of stock selection decisions made by branch staff? Many public library systems operate the former practice (and thus give line managers some useful experience of budgeting at an early stage in their careers), although Liddle seems to advocate the latter practice in stressing that stock selection should be kept separate from budget management:[9]

Many systems confuse the selection process with the essential budget monitoring process which must ensure that the budget is balanced to enable phased spending throughout the year. The budget monitoring process should be separate from the professional job of selection. Professional judgement should not be distorted by the availability or lack of money to spend. Librarians must select what they need. Whether or not they have it depends upon the person whose responsibility it is to control the budget.

In the academic library context, how should the library manager apportion funds for stock purchase between academic departments? Whatever simple or complex formula is adopted (student numbers, academic level of work, 'library-intensity' of courses, average cost of titles, useful shelf-life of knowledge, etc.), there will be complaints from departments which feel hard done by. At Birmingham Polytechnic, partly to alleviate this problem and partly to reduce central overheads and apportion expenditure to individual 'cost centres', the faculties are each given a notional amount for the library as part of their operating budget and they can then chose the actual amount they wish to spend on library stock. A proportion of what would have been the library's acquisitions budget has been, in effect, taken away from the library manager's control and handed over to the customer. It is that customer who then determines what amount will be spent on library stock as competing claims on the faculty's resources are reconciled.

Managing the book fund means dealing with library suppliers – commercial businesses which supply and process library stock to order. Because librarianship is a relatively small world, because many specialist suppliers employ professional librarians and show a genuine interest in issues of current concern, and because of the annual round of professional conferences attended by both librarians and 'the trade', a cosy and quite personal relationship can build up between library managers and the suppliers with whom they deal. Because of the Net Book Agreement (which fixes book prices and offers a standard discount for libraries), suppliers in the UK cannot compete on price. However, they can and do compete on performance – speed of supply, quality and variety of stock processing, bibliographic support for stock revision, booklists and approvals collections to support stock selection. It is, of course, the library manager's responsibility to make supply decisions on the basis of careful cost/benefit analysis.

The difficulties which library managers can experience in subdividing the acquisitions budget should give librarians some empathy with the difficulties experienced by the parent organization in allocating the overall budget between competing claimants, including the library. One of the important functions of the library's senior management is to acquire funds for the library by influencing decision-making in those arenas where the organization's total 'cake' is subdivided into individual 'slices'.

The amount of money spent on libraries may seem large, but in most organizations the library budget is, in fact, a very small part of the overall budget. Liddle suggests that public library spending accounts for just 1.5 per cent to 2.5 per cent of total expenditure in those UK local authorities which are responsible for an education service, and around 5 per cent of total expenditure in non-education authorities.[10] In UK universities and polytechnics, the library accounts for 4 per cent to 4.5 per cent of total expenditure.[11]

The relatively small size of these budgets can have advantages and disadvantages. On the one hand, the library service can be seen as relatively cheap and therefore as 'good value' for money: the Chief Executive of the UK Library Association is fond of noting that the public library service costs less than 'half a bar of chocolate' per person per week. It may also be the case that when a cut is needed in the overall budget, the library is left alone because a proportionate reduction in library spending would not produce any great saving in cash terms.

On the other hand, an 'across the board' cut in all budgets within the organization can have a disproportionately damaging effect on a department, like the library, which has only a small budget with which to work. It may also be difficult to get senior management within the parent organization to pay sufficient attention to library matters when the library's budget represents such a small proportion of the organization's overall financial activity. An education department may spend close to half of all the money spent by a UK local authority. If the Education Committee deals also with the library service (which spends between one per cent and two per cent of the authority's total expenditure), how much time will be given to library matters?

The amount of money given to libraries by their parent organization varies widely even amongst comparable institutions. In part, this may well relate to the character and quality of library management. Research into public libraries and their place within local authority structures has concluded that the nature and development of the service depends less on the organizational framework and more on the qualities of the Chief Librarian.[12] This reinforces the point (made in Chapter 2) that library managers need to get involved in decision-making at the

189

organizational level and promote the value of investment in the library.

Investment decisions are based on the perceived return, or 'payback', on that investment. That return may be in the form of actual income or some other tangible benefit, or some less visible but equally attractive outcome. The outcomes from library service are more likely to be 'invisible earnings' than tangible returns, and, for this reason, it is particularly important for the library's senior management to be aware of the political dimension of organizational decision-making (see Chapter 2). Library management can then use this dimension in stressing the payback on investments made in the library service. An academic institution, for example, might be interested in the library's contribution to student-centred learning (and a more efficient staff-student ratio). One local authority might be attracted by the library's potential to provide information support to local businesses; another by the library's potential to help redress disadvantage. A commercial corporation might be swayed by the idea that information provided by the library can contribute to competitive advantage. In each case, the library's senior management must find the appropriate 'political' argument by which to advance the library's case for adequate resources.

The enterprise approach
Faced with constraints on funds granted to the library by its parent organization, and with political pressure to be more entrepreneurial and less dependent on such granted funds, many library managers are seeking other sources of income. There are basically three types of alternative income source:

- grants from external funds: for example, public libraries in the UK have benefited from funding provided by the Manpower Services Commission, the Home Office, the various Arts Associations, the European Commission, and so on.[13]
- trading activities (for example, a library shop or publishing programme), including joint ventures between public-sector libraries and private-sector business.
- charging for library services: for example (as the UK green paper on public library financing suggests) defining the 'basic'

service, and levying a direct charge on customers using any 'additional' or 'specialized' service.

A discussion of the philosophical/ethical/political issues surrounding the 'fee, or free?' debate is beyond the scope of this book – except to note that library managers need to confront these issues and build them into the policy-making process. Of relevance here are the practical implications for library financial management of trading, charging, and the use of externally granted funds.

A key distinction between trading/charging activities and traditional library budgeting is that the latter is based on a fixed income (the eventual budget allocation for the year) while trading and charging imply that income will be variable, depending on the volume and price of services and products sold. Library managers may need to learn financial techniques designed to manage variable income and ensure that income is sufficient to meet expenditure.

For trading operations which are separated financially from the 'basic' library service, it may be necessary to prepare a *cashflow budget*. This itemizes estimated income and expenditure (usually on a month-by-month basis, projected forward for a year) in order to indicate net cash flow and ensure that the operation has enough cash in hand to cover its immediate liabilities. It may also be necessary, in pricing products and services, to use *break-even analysis* in order to determine the point at which a particular activity will cover its costs. To take the practical example of a library's publishing programme:

● A particular book incurs £1,000 in fixed costs (for example, cost of staff, building, etc.) and £5 per unit in variable costs (costs which vary with the volume of sales such as author's royalties or the unit cost of printing and distribution), assuming a sale of 200 copies. Given a selling price of £10 each, a simple calculation

$$\frac{\text{fixed operating costs}}{\text{(sale price per unit)} \quad - \quad \text{(variable cost per unit)}}$$

$$\frac{1000}{(10-5)} \quad = \quad \frac{1000}{5} \quad = \quad 200$$

191

indicates that if all 200 copies are sold the operation will break even.

This is a simplistic example, but it shows that careful analysis of fixed and variable costs, and finely judged decisions regarding price and likely volume of sales, are needed if library managers are to be successful as 'retailers' of products and services.

An important element in many of the processes described above is costing. The analysis of costs is central to: break-even analysis and cashflow budgeting; deliberations on charging for services; making the case for resources within the parent organization by demonstrating 'value for money'; choosing commercial suppliers; establishing joint ventures between public-sector libraries and private-sector business; the process of estimating likely expenditure; the development of any form of 'performance' budgeting.

Stephen Roberts comments that techniques of cost management are relatively underdeveloped in libraries,[14] but Roberts' own book on the subject (published in 1985), and the *Costing system for public libraries*[15] developed by CIPFA and published by the Office of Arts and Libraries in 1987, reflect an increasing focus on this subject in the UK. In the USA, the work of the PLA Cost Analysis Task Force and the ALA's publication in 1985 of *Cost finding for public libraries*[16] shows a similar focus of attention.

The CIPFA report, referring to public libraries, suggests that cost management has not been developed in the past because requirements for public accountability have not been so pressing. Library managers have tended to work with subjective and qualitative considerations more than objective measures, and no tradition has been built up of financial or managerial accountability. This is changing, and the report suggests that a costing system will enable library managers to:

- relate priority shifts to costs;
- develop more meaningful pricing policies;
- demonstrate exactly how much money is being spent on what services.

Similar points are made in the ALA's *Cost finding* handbook which emphasizes[17] that: 'More sharply focussed information is needed to justify budgetary requests, to initiate productivity improvements, to provide management with data on program and operational performance, and to support the variety of requests on decisions taken.'

The models developed by CIPFA and the ALA enable costs to be allocated to *cost centres* (that is, individual service points or support sections) and analysed by *functional areas* (that is, areas of service or support that cut across cost centres, such as 'reference services' or 'publicity'). CIPFA also explored the possibility of determining costs in relation to individual *'client groups'* and the report recommends further research into this approach.

There is a strong current interest in the UK in the development of a 'cost centre' approach to the financial management of library services. Traditionally, the line manager of a service unit has responsibility for a portion of the stock budget while most of the major costs associated with that unit are dealt with centrally by middle/senior management. A 'cost centre' approach would disaggregate central costs as much as possible, apportioning spending on staff, buildings, supplies, etc. to each service unit. Financial management (including decisions regarding local virement and the proportional expenditure on staff, stock, supplies, etc.) could then be devolved to the line manager of each service unit. This approach has already been implemented with regard to state-funded schools in the UK which are becoming largely autonomous in terms of financial management.

The CIPFA report points out that libraries do not have easily definable products or outputs which can be quantified, and that there is usually little financial expertise available within the library department itself. However it is a clear indication of the move towards a more precise accounting of costs in relation to activities – whether those activities are defined in terms of service points, support sections, functional areas, or customer groups.

A distinction can be drawn, then, between the traditional approach to library resourcing – with the library dependent for funds on its parent organization, and the budget related to previous expenditure – and the 'entrepreneurial' or 'enterprise' approach. This ties funding more closely to performance and, by diversifying sources of income, makes the library more self-reliant and less dependent on its parent organization. The characteristics of this approach are clear:

193

- 'Value for money': analysing and allocating costs, identifying outputs, and reviewing performance.
- 'Cost centres': devolving financial management to the level of individual service units.
- Competitive tendering: based on the proposition that it may, sometimes, be more efficient' to contract out a particular activity, *enabling* it to take place without directly *providing* it. Thus the client (for example, a library service) specifies costs, standards and targets for the activity being contracted out, and then monitors the contractor's performance.[18]
- Alternative funding strategies: attracting external funds, developing trading activities (including joint ventures), and charging for certain services.

Applying this approach may not make a considerable difference to libraries in purely financial terms. Library income is small in relation to expenditure and this will remain the case for the great majority of libraries. CIPFA figures (for 1985/6) show that, in England, public library income (£21.6m) covered just 5.2% of expenditure (£413.4m). If the notional target of £50m income, given in the UK government's green paper, were reached, this would still cover only 12% of the present level of expenditure. Most libraries will continue to remain, more or less, dependent on the budget granted to them by their parent organization.

But the size of that grant – the library's 'slice' of the organizational 'cake' – may well depend, in part, on the parent organization's perception of financial management within the library department. Library managers need to be able to present a strong and politically astute case for library resourcing. They need to prove that they can handle, creatively and successfully, the difficult operational decisions that follow when the allocated budget does not meet the estimates put forward. They need to demonstrate enterprise and accountability in their approach to financial management. They may then find it easier to convince those responsible for policy and resources that investment in the library service represents good value for money.

References

1   A full discussion of costing in relation to library service is given in

Stephen A. Roberts, *Cost management for library and information services*, Butterworths, 1985; and in Philip Rosenberg, *Cost finding for public libraries: a manager's handbook*, Chicago, ALA, 1985.

2 Both concepts are promoted in the green paper, *Financing our public library service: four subjects for debate* (Cm 324), HMSO, 1988. 'Joint ventures' are also the subject of OAL, *Joint enterprise: roles and relationships of the public and private sectors in the provision of library and information services*, Library Information Series no.16, HMSO, 1987.

3 CIPFA figures for 1985/6 give overall (actual) spending by public libraries in England as £413.4M, with capital spending accounting for £27.3M (6.60 per cent). SCONUL figures for the same year give overall spending by UK university libraries as £84.6M with capital spending accounting for £5.6M (6.62 per cent). Figures taken from the Appendices to *Report by the Minister for the Arts on Library and Information Matters during 1987*.

4 See John Blagden, 'Financial management: budgeting and costing' in L. J. Anthony (ed.), *Handbook of special librarianship and information work*, 5th edition, Aslib, 1982, pp.53 – 73.

5 David Liddle, *What the public library boss does*, AAL, 1985, p.11.

6 James Thompson and Reg Carr, *An introduction to university library administration*, 4th edition, LA, 1987, pp.27 – 8.

7 Guy St. Clair and Joan Williamson, *Managing the one-person library*, Butterworths, 1986, p.116.

8 Mary Jo Lynch, *Libraries in an information society: a statistical summary*, Chicago, ALA, June 1987.

9 Liddle, *What the public library boss does*, p.12.

10 *Ibid.*, p.23.

11 Figure derived from the SCONUL and COPOL data appended to *Report by the Minister for ... 1987*.

12 Margaret Lomer and Steve Rogers, *The public library and the local authority: organization and management*, BL R&D Report no.5738, Birmingham, Institute of Local Government Studies, University of Birmingham, 1983.

13 See Nick Moore and Elaine Kempson, *Financing development: the use of external funds by public libraries*, BL R&D Report no.5876, Bath, Parker Moore Ltd., 1986.

14 Roberts, *Cost management for library and informaton services*, p.2.

15 OAL, *A costing system for public libraries: a model system developed by Cipfa Services Ltd.*, Library Information Series no.17, HMSO, 1987.

16 Philip Rosenberg, *Cost finding for public libraries*, Chicago, ALA, 1985.

17 *Ibid.*, p.4.

18 A useful overview of the application of competitive tendering to UK local government is given by Norman Flynn and Kieron Walsh,

Competititve tendering, Birmingham, INLOGOV (Institute of Local Government Studies), University of Birmingham, 1988.

8 *Managing change*

Change and convergence
Libraries in both the UK and the USA are operating in a context of rapid and potentially discontinuous change.

- *Social change*: which changes peoples' needs and the uses that they make of libraries (particularly public libraries and some types of academic library); and therefore can change the nature of a library's purpose or 'mission', and its priorities for service delivery.
- *Technological change*: which changes the tools and systems with which librarians work; and is beginning (particularly in some academic and specialized libraries) to change the structures by which service is delivered.
- *Economic change*: which changes the extent and nature of the resources librarians have at their disposal; can change the approach of library management in response to pressure to be more accountable and entrepreneurial; and so can change attitudes to service delivery and priorities for service development.
- *Political change*: which links together all of the above in the process of making choices about policy, priorities, and resource allocations.

The forces for change are influencing the internal management dynamics of libraries and their parent organizations as well as the structure of service delivery and the nature of strategic thinking. This is evident in the key issues on which British and American management is focussing attention:

- *'Caring for the customer'*

This reflects a market-orientated approach to planning (target customer group, identify needs, develop services), and a concern for the quality of service delivery; particularly, the quality of personal contact and attention given to individual customers. Fundamental to this approach is good internal communications and an open and honest management style; the 'tick' of good internal relations leading to the 'click' of good relations between staff and customers.[1] Equally fundamental is a supportive attitude to staff, including training in 'customer care' techniques (listening skills, tone of voice and body language, assertiveness, etc.).

- *'Value for money'*

This reflects both the concern for customer satisfaction ('value' from the customer perspective), and the pressure for accountability ('value' from the resource-provider's perspective). From the customer perspective, there may be 'added value'[2] in services which are:

– specialist (either tailored to the individual customer, as is a consultancy service, or specialist rather than generalist in expertise and stock);

– timely (for example, using online technology to produce a speedier response);

– repackaged (whereby the librarian gathers, collates, evaluates and synthesizes the information on behalf of the customer);

– or tangible (that is, the customer owns the outcome – a report, FAX, photocopy, etc. – rather than borrowing the item or taking notes).

From the resource-provider's perspective, there is a need for performance indicators; and there may be a case, in the interests of efficiency, for contracting out elements of the service. In this situation, library management becomes the *enabling* force (setting standards, appointing contractors, monitoring performance, coordinating service) rather than *providing* all aspects of the service from in-house resources.

- *'Enterprise'*

By which the manager shows an enterprising (entrepreneurial, opportunistic) approach, both in attracting resources (through

198

alternative sources of funding, sponsorship, income generation, etc.) and also in providing service. It is important that both aspects of 'enterprise' are recognized. Being entrepreneurial is not simply about attracting funding; it is also about creative and innovative approaches to service. The UK Library Association's response to the green paper on public library finance, for example, illustrates with extracts from the *Library Association record* the many enterprising initiatives developed by UK public libraries within traditional financial and structural frameworks.[3]

Underlying the attention given to 'customer care', 'value for money', and 'enterprise' is a convergence of management approaches. The Audit Commission's checklist for a well-managed local authority, given in *The competitive council*, echoes the strategies of a commercial organization:[4]

- understand the customers;
- respond to the electorate;
- set and pursue consistent, achievable objectives;
- assign clear management responsibilities;
- train and motivate people;
- communicate effectively;
- monitor results;
- adapt quickly to change.

The attempt to simulate – and (through compulsory tender testing).stimulate – competition in previously non-commercial operations emphasizes the convergence of management approaches in the public (non-commercial and monopolistic) and private (commercial/competitive) sectors. Efficiency ('value for money' from the resource-provider's perspective), effectiveness ('value' and satisfaction from the customer's perspective), and 'enterprise' (in seeking resources and providing services) are the focus for managers in all types of organization.

In public-sector libraries – as in all other areas of public-sector activity – managers are beginning to apply business-sector processes while trying to achieve public-service outcomes. The next few years will be a particularly exciting and challenging time for public-sector library managers as this convergence of approaches is explored.

People and conflict

External social, economic and political change, and internal changes in technologies, service structures and management approaches all have an impact on the people working in the organization. The human aspects of change need to be as carefully planned as the technological or structural aspects.

All change is disruptive and stressful for those involved. Reactions can encompass a wide variety of attitudes:

- Antagonism: change is overtly resisted, or the fact of change is either denied or ignored.
- Acquiescence: this can take the form of a neutral ('wait and see') attitude, or a more negative response of withdrawal and non-involvement.
- Acceptance and adaptation: change is understood, anticipated, and planned for.

Feelings of antagonism or reluctant acquiescence will alter an individual's psychological contract with the workplace, diminishing any feeling of 'belonging', and reducing morale and motivation.

Good communications, consultation with those likely to be affected, and a constant flow of information as decisions are taken can help to produce a more positive attitude towards proposed changes. Managing change requires careful attention to *process* – the way in which things are done – as well as decisions about *outcomes* – the changes to be achieved. It is also important to anticipate the insecurity that people might feel in relation to a changed work situation, and to make it clear that staff will be fully supported – through training and counselling – during any transitional period.

However, this purely rational approach does not take full account of human nature. The absence of communication, explanation, and strategies for staff support will certainly produce a negative feeling; changes will be perceived as imposed, management will be seen as uncaring, and staff will have no sense of commitment to, or 'ownership' of, the decisions taken. But communication, explanation and support will not always produce a positive response. It may produce acceptance which is acquiescent rather than positively receptive. There may well be opposition based on vested interests, or a refusal to move away from existing 'custom and practice'.

Reluctance – or intransigence – in the face of change highlights one of the challenges of management. However much a manager wishes to support staff, build consensus, and exert power by influence, there will be times when he or she has no option but to exert the power of authority. A consultative/participative process is generally deemed preferable to an autocratic approach, but this 'softer' style does not mean that the manager becomes a 'soft touch'. The manager's responsibility is to carry out, firmly, the organization's objectives. It is important to recognize that the change process can involve conflict.

There are a number of ways in which a manager can respond to a conflict situation:

- avoidance: the manager refuses to confront the situation and make a decision.
- compromise: the manager accommodates the views of those who disagree with the original decision.
- problem-solving: the manager encourages those involved to explore the nature of the conflict and collaborate in finding a way forward.
- force: the manager imposes a solution using the power of authority.

The response used may well depend on the style and character of the individual manager. Ideally, it should depend on the particular situation. As with much in management, 'contingency theory' – that the action to be taken is contingent on the variables in each particular set of circumstances – applies. There are times when authority has to be exercised, however much this may breed resentment. There are times when conflict avoidance is a sensible strategy – giving a situation time to 'defuse' itself and become less heated and critical. There are times when compromise is necessary in order to move forward. There are times when an open discussion of the conflict situation – although it can be difficult to generate a suitably objective, reflective, and non-emotive exchange of views – can lead to a creative solution. What is important is that a manager:

- can recognize conflict;
- is not afraid to deal with it;

201

- has the flexibility and confidence to use a variety of approaches to conflict resolution, matching the approach to the particular situation.

Process and paradox

Dealing with conflict illustrates a paradox at the heart of management. A good manager should be supportive of staff, nurturing them and helping them to 'feel good' about themselves and the job. Sometimes, however, firm, authoritative action is required in the interests of the organization and its objectives. In working with staff, a manager has to be prepared to be tough as well as tender.

Just as there is a central paradox in the 'people' dimension of management, so there is a paradox at the core of the 'organizational' dimension – expressed in the concept of the 'loose-tight' organization. On the one hand is the 'looseness' of decentralization, delegation, and autonomy, encouraging independence, innovation and an entrepreneurial approach. On the other hand is the 'tightness' of centralized control, integration, and accountability. What is needed is balance: sufficient looseness and support for individuals and groups to 'go for it' without going overboard; sufficient tightness and control to ensure coherence of direction and an indication of progress, without inhibiting initiative by instilling a 'fear factor'.

Peters and Waterman promote organizational 'culture' as a way of resolving the 'loose-tight' paradox.[5] The looseness of autonomy and innovation is held together by tight allegiance and adherence to a set of core values constantly reinforced by a strong corporate culture. However, this creates a further paradox. A strong corporate culture may facilitate looseness and individual autonomy but it can also inhibit change. Shared values and a feeling for 'our way of doing things' can blinker people so that they do not see or accept alternative strategies or changed circumstances.

Managing change includes reinforcing and sustaining internal changes. Otherwise, initiatives introduced by individuals may fade and die when that individual moves on. One way to ensure this does not happen is to 'institutionalize' the changes made by incorporating them into the organization's structures. But then those changed structures may, in the future, become rigid strictures inhibiting further change.

What is needed is a corporate culture – and a framework of organizational structures – which looks outward rather than inward, forward rather than back, and which can anticipate, plan for, and accommodate change.

Avoiding entropy

How, then, can library managers meet the challenge of change? What management approaches might assist in making libraries 'high performance' units, looking outward and forward? The search for corporate 'excellence' gives some clues, producing a checklist which can be applied as much to libraries as to any type of organization. The concepts are essentially the same in the British and American literature; the headings below are those used by Goldsmith and Clutterbuck:[6]

- Leadership: visible top management, clear objectives which are understood throughout the organization, and an environment in which managers at all levels can lead.
- Autonomy: decentralization, minimum bureaucracy, a positive attitude towards risk-taking, and an environment in which managers are encouraged to exercise initiative (within a clear framework of permissible activity).
- Control: maintaining a balance between control and autonomy/flexibility by strong financial management, close attention to planning, constant feedback on results, a long-term perspective with a clear sense of where the organization is going, and high standards that people are expected to keep to.
- Involvement: building commitment in people through a number of strategies: high pay and incentives; stress on promotion from within; creation of pride in ownership either through real ownership (giving staff a financial share in the company) or through a high level of consultation and discussion which makes people feel they have a 'stake' in the organization; high levels of information flow in relation to individual job performance and each individual's role in relation to the organization as a whole; stress on training; recognition of the importance of the social side of work.
- Market orientation: detailed research and close interaction with the market, constant quality control, with customer

satisfaction the prime objective in all aspects of the
organization's work.
- Zero basing, or, keeping in close touch with the basics of
the business: sticking with fundamentals both in the nature
of the business (not diversifying away from the core business
area) and in attention to the detail of the business.
- Innovation: continuous interest in new things (including
curiosity about what is going on outside the organization),
with low internal barriers to change.
- Integrity: the organization is perceived as fair, honest and
even-handed by staff, customers, suppliers, and the wider
community.

Underlying this checklist are three key points: organizational
development; support for staff; and the importance of *process* as
well as *outcomes*.

Entropy – loss of energy, 'running out of steam' – can affect
organizations as much as any other form of system. Organizations
have a natural tendency towards bureaucracy and inertia. Like
humans, they can become flabby and slow unless positive steps
are taken to keep them in trim. Organizational development –
the process of innovation and renewal – is the equivalent of
physical exercise; it helps organizations to keep in shape and avoid
entropy.

But being innovative does not just mean doing something –
anything – that is entirely new. The concept of 'innovation' must
be linked to that of 'zero basing'. Literally, innovation implies
a process of renewal, and the successful organization 'renews'
itself while continuing to stick closely to its fundamental purpose.

There is a difficulty here for some libraries. It is all very well
for Peters and Waterman[7] to cry 'stick to the knitting' (that is,
remain true to the organization's fundamental purpose) – but
do all libraries know what their 'knitting' is? Public libraries on
both sides of the Atlantic have always had a somewhat loose and
diffuse concept of purpose: as a force for education, information,
culture and recreation in the local community. At a time of
economic constraint when choices have to be made about purpose
and priorities, this rather vague sense of mission is not enough.
A public library service may have to confront the need to make
a choice: recreation *or* information *or* education *or* culture? This

need to choose a role lies behind the work of the ALA's Public Library Development Program on planning and role-setting.[8] Similarly, an academic library may have to choose between support for teaching (multiple copies of texts, high turnover of stock) *or* for research (single copies of many items, collection building). In some organizations within the commercial sector these choices have already been made with distinctions between the library (an archival role), records management (control of internal documentation), and market intelligence or research and development (synthesizing current information from external sources). A necessary but sometimes difficult first step towards innovation and renewal is for the library to define its purpose in relation to the customer community.

A number of considerations can help to develop an organizational culture which looks outward and forward – a culture of innovation and renewal:

- Management style: leaders set the tone and focus the attention of an organization; managers express a visible interest in innovation.
- Forward planning: the networks of consultation and decision-making within the organization are future focussed. Meetings are not bogged down in bureaucracy. Agendas are seen as opportunities to discuss key issues, not to transact routine items of administration. The free flow of ideas is encouraged, using techniques to stimulate creative and lateral thinking.
- Organizational structure: the structure is flat and organic rather than tall and hierarchical, encouraging people to communicate and contribute; people move around the organization rather than ossifying into one position.
- Outward looking: the organization has a wide-ranging external perspective. In a library this might be encouraged and reflected by involvement with outside bodies, attendance at conferences, the circulation of reports, journals, etc.
- Research: within the organization there are a number of 'action research' projects directed towards organizational objectives. A UK public library, for example, might be involved in a local Library and Information Plan, be introducing a new service supported by the government's Public Library Development Incentive Scheme, be carrying

205

out some form of market research (perhaps using librarian-ship students as market researchers), or be experimenting at a number of individual service points with new forms of stock arrangement or service delivery. Adding a research dimension to the internal dynamics of the organization immediately focusses attention on innovation and the future.

- Technology: the introduction of new technology brings innovation in organizational processes (acquisitions, cataloguing, circulation control, interlending, etc.) and in customer services (videotex, online searching, CD-ROM, etc.).

This focus on development, innovation, and renewal needs to be reflected in the way that staff are supported. Good communications are essential to keep everybody informed about what is going on. A management style that is participative – with that culture of participation permeating all levels of the organization – will encourage people to feel involved with new developments. A programme of staff training will help people feel that they can cope with changing circumstances and priorities. An appraisal system – if viewed in a positive light and conducted with integrity – can provide a valuable means of helping individuals to 'grow' within the organization by identifying and discussing opportunities for development in terms of job-related skills and attributes, management experience, or personal maturity.

In the context of libraries it is particularly important to remember:

- that library assistants are in the front line of customer service. They need to be fully integrated into any strategies for training, development, or building a sense of involvement with the organization as a whole.
- that librarians are expert in a range of specialist techniques, not in the skills of management. They need to be supported – through training, counselling and coaching – as they take on management responsibilities. This is particularly important in a decentralized library system in which librarians at a fairly early career stage can find themselves in crucial line management positions (as branch librarians, subject librarians, section heads, etc.) forming a vital link between the

206

managerial/professional echelons and a group of library assistants.

- that senior staff still need training and opportunities for development in order to retain their capacity for action, awareness and leadership.

Injecting a development dimension into organizational dynamics and building a supportive environment for staff requires careful attention to *process*:

- The human/social processes by which people work and interact together.
- The technical/bureaucratic processes through which organizations structure their activities and determine their priorities for attention and action.

When considering change – either the impact of external change, or the dynamics of internal change – managers need to reflect on both 'people' and 'organizational' considerations:

- people: recruitment and selection strategies; training and development programmes; reward systems; leadership styles.
- organization: authority-responsibility relationships; communication networks; work-flows and composition of work groups; applications of technology to operational processes.

As well as focussing on the future and planning for change, managers have to be alive to the present and the need to achieve optimum efficiency and effectiveness in day-to-day operations. All this requires considerable powers of reflection and intuition, allied to an eye for detail and an awareness of the importance of 'casual' encounters in reinforcing opinions and attitudes. A crucial element in management, then, is thinking – about external change, organizational development, staff support, internal dynamics and processes.

Yet, the stereotypes of 'managing' and 'thinking' seem opposed. 'Managing' is active, practical, collective. 'Thinking' – like the Rodin statue of 'The Thinker' – is passive, inward-looking, individual. However, much thinking is, in fact, highly collective and interactive – in meetings, conversations, arguments, 'buzz' groups and 'brainstorming' sessions. Managers need to stimulate and develop both types of thinking: collective decision-thinking within the organization, and individual reflection on processes and strategies. Finding time to think – including time out of working hours – is an important part of successful management.[9]

Thinking requires information, and increasing attention is being given to the use of information as a resource by management. A flow of accurate, timely and relevant information is crucial to the processes of planning, implementation and control. 'Information management' – or, in computing circles, 'strategic information systems planning' (SISP) – is emerging as a key area of management development.[10] In librarianship this is reflected by interest in management information systems (MIS), and by the associated search for appropriate 'performance indicators' to be fed into such a system. Three principles should guide the development of any MIS:

- Information should not be collected unless it is useful to, and used by, those for whom it is collected.
- The information collected should be useful to those by whom it is collected; otherwise they will have no 'stake' in ensuring its availability and accuracy.
- A simple system which is easy to operate and broadly indicative is more use than a complex system which is comprehensive, detailed, and unworkable.

Libraries need to recognize these principles if the theoretic models of 'performance indicator' sets currently being developed are to be put, usefully, into practice. Peters and Waterman write of 'a bias for action'.[11] Performance measurement (or rather, performance *review*) is one of those areas where librarianship has shown a bias towards inaction by endlessly discussing theory rather than getting on with implementation.

For library managers – as for many managers in both public and private sectors – the classic management cycle of planning, implementation, and control has become a rigorous process of

- making and justifying choices;
- setting objectives and achieving targets;
- demonstrating efficiency, effectiveness, and enterprise;
- evaluating individual and organizational performance.

In the UK, for many libraries, this rigorous process is set into a context of intense political activity. Libraries are on the political agenda – caught in the crossfire between ideologies with conflicting views on the role, structure, and funding of the public sector. At a time of constrained funding and competing demands, libraries in all types of organizations are caught up in the process of institutional politics by which priorities are set and resources allocated. The choices made by a library's senior management are often, of necessity, conditioned by this political dimension. To handle the managerial/political process successfully, a manager needs strength of character, an awareness of key issues and techniques, time to think, and relevant information.

For library managers, the way forward is partly indicated by the nature of librarianship itself. Traditionally, libraries are about communal, collective action; the community buys books to be shared by individual borrowers. Libraries are also about sociable and socializing experiences; the human interaction between staff and users is important in defining job satisfaction and the quality of service experienced by the customer. Libraries are also about the management of information; knowledge is organized for retrieval and use. Increasingly, libraries are also about the dissemination of information; enterprising innovations in service (SDI services, user education programmes, community information provision, etc.) show the library marketing itself, pro-actively, to the customer community. Ultimately, an effective library is one which brings together an outward-looking concern for customer service, and an inward-looking attention to the detail of operational systems.

Management, too, is about these activities:

- collective action; through good communications, participative decision-making structures, and an open management style.
- human interaction; through formal and informal methods of supporting staff so that they 'feel good' about themselves and their work.
- information management; through mechanisms for feedback from customers (surveys, etc.), staff (group meetings, one-to-one appraisal sessions, etc.), and data on services and systems (financial control systems, MIS, etc.).
- a pro-active approach; through structures which support

enterprise and the process of innovation and renewal, within a defined framework of purpose and objectives.

- attention to detail; by thinking through all of the above so that the culture (collective, supportive, evaluative, innovative) is reinforced by the 'small stuff' of day-to-day activities and exchanges, and is not merely given lip-service in policy statements and management meetings.

The principles and approaches of modern librarianship are exactly those needed by modern management. In today's organizational climate of enterprise and accountability, managers at all levels need to develop processes and strategies which are collective, supportive, evaluative, and innovative. The aim of this book is to stimulate thinking about these processes and strategies amongst library managers.

References

1 Sue Fontaine, *Public relations in public libraries: report to the Council on Library Resources*, 1975; noted in Bob Usherwood, *The visible library; practical public relations for public librarians*, LA, 1983, p.113.
2 Robert S. Taylor, *Value-added processes in information systems*, Ablex Publishing Corporation, Norwood, New Jersey, 1986, analyses the 'value-added' spectrum of activities in a way which correlates directly with the core functions of librarians.
3 *The Library Association's response to 'Financing our Public Library Service: Four Subjects for Debate' Cm 324*, LA, June 1988.
4 Audit Commission, *The competitive council*, Management Paper no.1, March 1988.
5 Peters and Waterman, *In search of excellence*, p.318f.
6 Goldsmith and Clutterbuck, *The winning streak*, Penguin, 1985.
7 Peters and Waterman, *In search of excellence*, p.292f.
8 C. R. McClure *et al.*, *Planning and role setting for public libraries*, Chicago, ALA, 1987.
9 See Ben Heirs, with Peter Farrell, *The professional decision-thinker: our new management priority*, Sidgwick and Jackson, 1986.
10 See R. I. Tricker, *Effective information management: developing information systems strategies*, Oxford, Beaumont Executive Press, 1982; or Forest Woody Horton and Donald Marchand (eds.), *Information management in public administration*, Arlington, Information Resources Press, 1982.
11 Peters and Waterman, *In search of excellence*, p.119f.

Further reading

The aim of this section is to bring together some of the books noted in the text (adding a few titles which have not been mentioned earlier) to help any reader who wishes to explore issues in greater detail. The list of titles is not exhaustive but merely indicative; it is intended to provide a starting point for further study. Place of publication is London unless otherwise stated. In the main, British editions are cited because they are the ones consulted by the author.

Management

Peter Drucker, *The practice of management*, Heinemann, 1955.

is a classic text which still provides a valuable overview, introducing many ideas which remain the common currency of management literature. More recent introductions, designed specifically for those who are fairly new to management studies or managerial responsibility are:

Peter Lawrence, *Invitation to management*, Oxford, Blackwell, 1986.

Peter Lawrence and Ken Elliott (eds.), *Introducing management*, Penguin, 1985.

Rosemary Stewart, *The reality of management*, 2nd edition, Heinemann, 1985.

The classic study of the ways in which managers actually spend their time is:

Henry Mintzberg, *The nature of managerial work*, New York, Harper and Row, 1973.

and this focus on the 'real life' activities of managers is also reflected in:

Peter Lawrence, *Management in action*, Routledge and Kegan Paul, 1984.

An illuminating exploration of the element of choice and discretion in managerial work is provided by:

Rosemary Stewart, *Choices for the manager: a guide to managerial work and behaviour*, McGraw-Hill, 1982.

All facets of the relationship between people and organizations are examined thoroughly and fluently in:

Charles B. Handy, *Understanding organizations*, Penguin, 3rd edition, 1985.

The current concern for 'enterprise' is anticipated in:

Peter Drucker, *Innovation and entrepreneurship: practice and principles*, Pan/Heinemann, 1986.

A number of 'pop' management books provide useful insights as well as easy reading and interesting anecdotes. The key theories of successful staff management are condensed into a few pithy aphorisms in:

Kenneth Blanchard and Spenser Johnson, *The one minute manager*, Fontana/Collins, 1983.

A consistent checklist for 'excellent' organizational performance emerges from:

Thomas J. Peters and Robert H. Waterman, *In search of excellence: lessons from America's best-run companies*, New York, Harper and Row, 1982.

Tom Peters and Nancy Austin, *A passion for excellence: the leadership difference*, Fontana/Collins, 1986.

Walter Goldsmith and David Clutterbuck, *The winning streak: Britain's top companies reveal their formulas for success*, Penguin, 1985.

Types of library
Many books that are relevant to library management deal with one particular type of library. Current public library issues are raised in:

Colin Harris and Brian Clifford (eds.), *Public libraries: reappraisal and restructuring*, Rossendale, 1985.

Bob McKee, *Public libraries – into the 1990s?*, AAL Publishing, 1987.

Alphonse F. Trezza (ed.), *Public libraries and the challenges of the next two decades*, Littleton, Colorado, Libraries Unlimited Inc., 1985.

Academic libraries are the focus of:

Tim Lomas (ed.), *Management issues in academic libraries*, Rossendale, 1986.

James Thompson and Reg Carr, *An introduction to university library administration*, 4th edition, LA, 1987.

John Cowley (ed.), *The management of polytechnic libraries*, Gower/COPOL, 1985.

The work of library user education is set into the management cycle of planning and evaluation in:

Patricia Senn Breivik, *Planning the library instruction program*, Chicago, ALA, 1982.

Some of the current strategic issues facing academic libraries – particularly the interrelation of information services and information technology – are discussed in:

Campus of the future: conference on information resources; Wingspread Conference Center, June 22–24, 1986, Dublin, Ohio, OCLC, 1987.

The most useful overview of work in specialized library and information units is provided by:

L. J. Anthony (ed.), *Handbook of special library and information work*, 5th edition, Aslib, 1982.

Many librarians work in one-person libraries where the whole range of managerial responsibilities becomes the task of a single professional librarian.

Janet Shuter, *The information worker in isolation: problems and achievements*, Bradford, MCB Publications, 1984.

analyses the difficulties and satisfactions in this type of work, while

Guy St. Clair and Joan Williamson, *Managing the one-person library*, Butterworths, 1986

provides an overview from the management perspective.

Beth Wheeler Fox, *The dynamic community library: creative, practical, and inexpensive ideas for the Director*, Chicago, ALA, 1988

gives an enthusiastic and useful guide to the challenges of running a small community library.

Planning library service

The most valuable books in this area have come from the Public Library Association, a division of the American Library Association, and stem from the PLA's 'Public Library Development Program'. The Program comprises work in three main areas:

- planning and role setting.
- output measurement.
- the development of a national (US) Public Library Data Service.

Although the frame of reference is public libraries – and the United States – the principles are universally applicable:

Vernon E. Palmour *et al.*, *A planning process for public libraries*, Chicago, ALA, 1980.

Nancy A. Van House *et al.*, *Output measures for public libraries: a manual of standardized procedures*. 2nd edition, Chicago, ALA, 1987. This is a revised edition of Douglas Zweizig, *Output measures for public libraries*, ALA, 1982 – although the measures used remain unchanged in the two editions.

C. R. McClure *et al.*, *Planning and role setting for public libraries: a manual of options and procedures*, Chicago, ALA, 1987.

Managing library staff
A good overview of this area is provided by:

Noragh Jones and Peter Jordan, *Staff management in library and information work*, Gower, 2nd edition, 1987.

John Cowley, *Personnel management in libraries*, Bingley, 1982.

There are many books covering particular aspects of this subject, such as:

Don Revill (ed.), *Personnel management in polytechnic libraries*, Gower/COPOL, 1987.

Mark Shields, *Work and motivation in academic libraries*, Bradford, MCB University Press, 1988.

Gillian Burrington, *Equal opportunities in librarianship? Gender and career aspirations*, LA, 1987.

David Baker, *What about the workers? A study of non-professional staff in library work*, AAL Pointers series no.4, AAL Publications, 1986.

Sheila D. Creth, *Effective on-the-job training: developing library human resources*, Chicago, ALA, 1986.

Judith W. Powell and Robert B. LeLieuvre, *Peoplework: communications dynamics for librarians*, Chicago, ALA, 1979.

Anne J. Mathews, *Communicate! A librarian's guide to interpersonal relations*, Chicago, ALA, 1983.

Libraries and organizational structures

Two books which look at a range of issues in library management are useful on issues of organizational structure:

Sheila Ritchie (ed.), *Modern library practice*, 2nd edition, Kings Ripton, ELM Publications, 1982.

Ken Jones, *Conflict and change in library organizations: people, power, and service*, Bingley, 1984.

From an American perspective:

Robert D. Stueart and John Taylor Eastlick, *Library management*, 2nd edition, Littleton, Colorado, Libraries Unlimited Inc., 1981

examines the organizational dynamics of libraries and discusses library management in the context of the classic 'management cycle' of planning, organizing, staffing, directing, and controlling.

Libraries and information technology

There are a large number of books dealing with IT applications in libraries, although there is little, as yet, which focusses specifically on the management aspects and implications.

Jenny Rowley, *Info-tech: a guide for young professional librarians*, AAL Pointers series no.5, Association of Assistant Librarians, 1987

provides a useful survey of the 'new' technologies currently applied to library work, while

Ian Lovecy, *Automating library procedures: a survivor's handbook*, LA, 1984

gives a valuable and practical survey, based on personal experience, of the challenges involved in installing an automated library system.

A sensible overview of the current (or, at least, fairly recent) state of IT applications in large libraries is given by:

The state of the art of the application of new information technologies in libraries and their impact on library functions (EUR 11036), Luxembourg, Commission of the European Communities, Directorate-General for Telecommunications, Information Industries and Innovation, 1987. Reports have been issued for each of the 12 member states of the European Community. UK report available from: The Library and Information Technology Centre, Polytechnic of Central London, 235 High Holborn, London WC1B 4DF.

A companion study, focussing on North American networks, is:

Charles Hildreth, *Library automation in North America: a re-assessment of the impact of new technologies on networking*, (EUR 11092), Munich, K. G. Saur, 1987.

Library management: the 'control' function
The classic study of this area is:

F. W. Lancaster, *The measurement and evaluation of library services*, Washington DC, Information Resources Press, 1977

which has been recently complemented by:

F. W. Lancaster, *If you want to evaluate your library . . .* , Graduate School of Library and Information Science, University of Illinois (USA), and LA Publishing (UK), 1988.

Questions of cost/benefit and performance measurement are also raised in:

John Blagden, *Do we really need libraries?*, Bingley, 1980.

Management information systems are the subject of:

Peter Brophy, *Management information and decision-support systems in libraries*, Gower, 1986

Colin Harris (ed.), *Management information systems in libraries and information services*, Taylor Graham, 1988.

The concern on both sides of the Atlantic for costing service is reflected in:

Stephen Roberts, *Cost management for library and information services*, Butterworths, 1985

Philip Rosenberg, *Cost finding for public libraries: a manager's handbook*, Chicago, ALA, 1985

while the concern to identify benefits ('value' from the customer perspective) is reflected in:

National Consumer Council, *Measuring up: consumer assessment of local authority services: a guideline study. Paper 3: public libraries*, NCC, 1986.

Methods and mechanisms for gaining feedback from the customer community are the subject of:

Sue Stone, *Library surveys*, 2nd revised edition, Bingley, 1982.

A useful case study of the application of performance review techniques to library management (in the context of a UK public library) is provided by:

Graham Combe (ed.), *Performance review in the library service: the Surrey experience*, Public Libraries Research Group, 1987.

Libraries: image and expectation
Feedback can be subjective, conditioned by expectations. Margaret Slater has carried out a number of research studies which touch on the image of libraries and librarians, for example:

Margaret Slater, *Non-use of library-information resources at the workplace*, Aslib, 1984.

The importance of public relations and service presentation is stressed in many texts. Useful UK-based discussions of this topic are contained in:

Roger Stoakley, *Presenting the library service*, Bingley, 1982.

Bob Usherwood, *The visible library: practical public relations for public librarians*, LA, 1983

Bob Usherwood (ed.), *Professional persuasion: library public relations and promotion*, Association of Assistant Librarians, 1983

Margaret Kinnell, *Planned public relations for libraries: a PPRG handbook*, Taylor Graham, 1988.

Libraries: the UK governing framework
There is no single government minister or office responsible for all aspects of UK library service. The Minister for Arts and Libraries (supported by the Office of Arts and Libraries) has a responsibility to Parliament for those library services which are linked directly to legislation: public libraries and the British Library. These responsibilities are reflected in:

Report by the Minister for the Arts on Library and Information Matters, issued annually as a House of Commons paper by HMSO.

The annual review of library and information services by the Library and Information Services Council and the statistical appendices (both included with the Minister's annual report) give a wider view, including data on polytechnics and universities.

In 1988, the UK government issued a consultative 'green paper'

Financing our Public Library Service: Four Subjects for Debate, Cm 324, HMSO, 1988

raising issues of fundamental importance to public-sector library managers: wider charging for services as a means of generating new money for growth and development; joint ventures with private-sector agencies as a means of providing better and more effective services; contracting out to competitive tender as a means to better and more cost-effective services.

Current government and management issues are also reflected in the 'Library Information Series' of publications produced by the Office of Arts and Libraries. Three titles with particular relevance to current concerns are:

219

The future development of libraries and information services: progress through planning and partnership; report by the Library and Information Services Council, Library Information Series No.14, HMSO, 1986.

Joint enterprise: roles and relationships of the public and private sectors in the provision of library and information services; report by the Library and Information Services Council and British Library Research and Development Department Working Party, Library Information Series No.16, HMSO, 1987.

A costing system for public libraries: a model system developed by Cipfa Services Ltd (in conjunction with the Institute of Public Finance Ltd), Library Information Series No.17, HMSO, 1987.

The focus of these three reports – on planning, enterprise, and accountability – is a useful indication of the current framework within which library managers, in all types of organizations, have to work.

It is interesting to note that these reports emanate from a government department, while in the USA reports on similar topics (planning, costing, etc.) have emerged from the profession itself – from the American Library Association.

In the UK it is an interventionist and energetic government which is setting the agenda and showing 'a bias for action'. In the USA, the profession's own association retains the initiative and shows the way forward.

Government in the USA may well take a lead, in terms of economic policy, from its UK counterpart. Librarians in the UK may well have something to learn from the pro-active and positive approach of colleagues in the USA. Clearly, the so-called 'special relationship' between Britain and America has reverberations for library managers as well as government politicians.

Index

Chartered Institute of Public
Finance and Accountancy
(CIPFA) 158, 160 – 1, 181,
194
Cleveland 162
'closed' (cf. 'open') communities
26 – 7, 49, 55
Clutterbuck, David (with Walter
Goldsmith) 85, 203 – 4
Clwyd 3
coaching 105 – 7
collection development 131
communication 39, 73, 74, 77,
87 – 92, 145
community information 142
community librarianship 72
community profiling 55
competitive tendering 10, 74,
183, 194
conflict 201
contingency theory 70 – 1, 116,
201
contracting out 73, 198
Cornford, F. M. 40 – 1
corporate identity 60 – 1
cost-benefit analysis 147, 177
cost centre 23, 183, 193 – 4
costing 9, 182, 192
Council of Polytechnic Librarians
(COPOL) 160 – 1, 172 – 4,
186
counselling 8, 105 – 7, 145
Cowley, John 41, 107, 116, 125
crisis management 29
culture 80 – 5
  customer care 60
  enterprise culture 3, 8
  library image 57
  'loose-tight' 31, 80, 202
  organizational dynamics 7
  'structuring' and 'supporting'
  107 – 8
customer
  choice 2
  as consumer 2, 52
  library image 57
  organizational culture 60

public relations 62
staff attitudes 18, 59 – 60, 98
technology 131 – 2, 139,
142 – 4
customer care 60, 198
customer community
  deinstitutionalization 118
  goodwill 41
  marketing 48
  'open' and 'closed' communities
  26 – 7, 49, 55
customer complaints 169
customer feedback 55 – 6
customer requirements 1, 54
cybernetics 70

data collection 55, 155, 158
data comparison 159 – 60
decentralization 4, 16, 72, 75,
79, 117, 203
decision making 34 – 40, 115
deference 117
deinstitutionalization 118
delegation 17, 19, 25
Department of Education and
Science (DES) 120
deskilling 145
directorates 71
disciplinary procedure 37
discontinuous change 4, 31, 55,
82, 197
division of work 76 – 7
Drucker, Peter 13, 15, 22, 36,
69, 86, 109

education; of librarians 18,
58, 119, 122
electronic mail 90, 131
electronic text transfer 135
enabling (cf. providing) 74, 198
enterprise 3, 8, 80, 179, 190 – 4,
198 – 9
entropy 203 – 8
equal opportunities 23, 30, 37,
120 – 1
European Commission 3, 133 – 4,
139, 190

222

225